TURFGRASS
ECOLOGY &
MANAGEMENT

BY T. KARL DANNEBERGER, Ph.D

TURFGRASS
ECOLOGY&
MANAGEMENT

By T. Karl Danneberger, Ph.D

Cindy Code, Editor
and Co-Publisher of
Lawn & Landscape Maintenance
Magazine

Editor: Cindy Code
Cover and Interior Book Design: Charlotte Turcotte
Layout and Production: Helen Duerr O'Halloran
Desktop Coordinator: Christopher W. Foster
Production Manager: Jami Childs
Books Manager: Fran Franzak

If you have any questions or comments concerning this book, please write:
    Franzak & Foster
    G.I.E. Inc., Publishers
    4012 Bridge Ave.
    Cleveland, OH 44113

Library of Congress Catalog Card Number: 93-78045

ISBN 1-883751-00-4 hardcover

Table of Contents

About the Author

T. Karl Danneberger is an associate professor of turfgrass science at The Ohio State University, Columbus. Dr. Danneberger received his B.S. degree in Agronomy from Purdue University, West Lafayette, Ind., his M.S. degree from the Department of Horticulture at the University of Illinois, Urbana, and his Ph.D. degree in Plant Pathology from Michigan State University, E. Lansing.

Dr. Danneberger is responsible for the undergraduate turfgrass management program at The Ohio State University. His academic research specialization is in the area of turfgrass management. For the past 10 years, Dr. Danneberger has conducted research in the area of plant stress physiology, seed physiology, nutrient fate, localized dry spots, cultural programs for turfgrass systems and the development of disease prediction and plant growth models. Dr. Danneberger has served as a technical adviser to a number of turfgrass trade organizations and publications, as well as served as a speaker at numerous turfgrass conferences.

Dr. Danneberger is a member of the American Society of Agronomy, International Turfgrass Society and the Association for the Advancement of Science. He is a member of the Gamma Sigma Delta Honorary Society and has received the Outstanding Teaching Award from The Ohio State University College of Agriculture.

Dedicated to my wife and two sons:

Sallie A.
Marc T.
Kyle J.

Preface

THIS BOOK was written for the advanced turfgrass student and the practicing turfgrass manager. It was not written to compete with other turfgrass management books on the market, but to supplement them. It is hoped that the principles applicable to turfgrass management and the examples used in this book are of practical importance. Perhaps most importantly, it is the mission of this book to stimulate the turfgrass manager to develop a working philosophy of complete turfgrass management.

As you read through this book, refer to the glossary which is provided to supply a quick means of defining terms not yet discussed, or as a reminder of concepts previously covered. Additionally, you'll find color photos and figures throughout each chapter. Tables which are referred to in the text are found at the end of each chapter.

I wish to recognize and thank the following reviewers who provided me with a comprehensive critique of portions of this book: Donald Eckert, Emilie Regnier, William Pound, Michael Lauer, Edward McCoy, Miller McDonald Jr., William Shane, John Gasper and Mary Lush. I would also like to thank my editor, Cindy Code; cover and interior book designer, Charlotte Turcotte; layout and production Helen Duerr O'Halloran; desktop coordinator, Chris Foster; production manager, Jami Childs; and everyone associated with this book at G.I.E. Publishing. And finally, I would like to thank Richard Naughtin, William Daniel, Alfred Turgeon and Joseph Vargas Jr. for their indelible impression on how I think about turf.

Introduction
Ecology:
The Framework for
Turfgrass Management

*It is possible to fly without motors,
but not without knowledge and skill.
— Wilbur Wright, Inventor*

WHY WRITE THIS book when there are so many excellent turfgrass books on the market? A fair enough question. My answer involves addressing three concerns that are critical to the future of the green industry.

The first is to provide an overall framework by which to look at turfgrass management. Turfgrass management as a profession faces new challenges. Questions regarding environmental concerns such as the fate of pesticides and nutrients, and water use continue to be asked. As turfgrass managers, do we see enough of the big picture to reply? For example, one beneficial aspect of properly maintained turf is the oxygen which turf provides. As plants die and clippings decompose, the byproduct of microbial respiration is carbon dioxide. So what is the net contribution? What impact does bagging and disposing of clippings have on the net effect of carbon cycling?

This example may seem trivial, but more complex agronomic questions require an understanding of turfgrass, the turfgrass ecosystem and the mass flow of energy through the system.

A second reason for writing this book is the challenge of maintaining quality turf more efficiently. A revolution in management practices has occurred over the last 15 years in the overall quality of turf. Previously, only a select few home lawns or golf courses were maintained at the highest management intensity. Often, the limiting factors for achieving the superior home lawn or best playing golf course were expertise and money. Now, with more trained professionals and increased monetary inputs, highly maintained turf is widespread. In the future, what will separate the best professionals from the rest?

The ability of turfgrass managers to deliver high quality turf at all levels has resulted in high expectations of the user (e.g., golfers, homeowners, athletes and fans). In light of increasing public expectations, the turfgrass industry is trying to address issues such as limited resource availability (e.g., water shortages in the western United States) and the public perception of high pesticide and nutrient use causing public health problems. Despite recent advancements, some experts predict the future of turfgrass management will consist of lower quality turf resulting in lower public expectations. It is my opinion that unless there is a socioeconomic change resulting in turning back the clock, expectations will not change.

The ability to deliver high quality turfgrass with less inputs will require greater efficiency by the turfgrass manager. To meet this challenge, turfgrass managers will require more than technical expertise of how something is done, but an understanding of proper turfgrass selection and what effects a cultural or chemical practice have on the turfgrass ecosystem. This ability will separate the best from the rest.

The third reason for this book is to explain the concepts behind common management practices. Currently, turfgrass managers have the technical skills, but may lack the fundamental knowledge of why these practices are done. An understanding is particularly important because turfgrass management is a big business with complex problems. Because of the technical nature of "managing" a turfgrass system, research—whether by a scientist or turfgrass manager—is required to answer these problems.

The most widely used research approach is pragmatic and empirical in nature. In other words, practical problems are solved by asking a focused technical question and then conducting the experiments to find the answer. It's difficult to argue with the results of this approach especially when you visit a highly manicured turf such as a golf course, athletic field or home lawn. However, with the increased bombardment of new products, opinions and information in general, pitfalls exist with a pragmatic approach to problem solving.

Syndon in the book "Amenity Grasslands" succinctly stated this concern when he warned:

"Without the basis of a dynamic conceptual framework, there is a danger that this empirical and pragmatic approach may degenerate into a body of dogma (i.e., asserting an opinion as if it were fact). The danger is heightened by a constant demand to provide quick answers to practical problems, usually on the basis of inadequate information."

The framework for turfgrass management is the discipline of ecology. Ecology deals with individuals, communities and the environment, as well as interactions between them. Ecological studies focus on the defining principles encompassing numerous organisms, with considerably less attention paid to solving specific problems. Theory will not instantaneously provide ways of maintaining a putting green at less than 1/8 inch in 95 degree heat. However, theory provides a means of

8

explaining, and thus predicting, community events which then suggest ways of manipulating the community through management practices.

This book is broken down into two main categories. The first deals with resources and conditions. Resources are materials that are consumed and are most likely limiting to turfgrass growth. The capture of energy (photosynthesis), gases (carbon dioxide and oxygen), water, nutrition and soil are explained and discussed. Space is also a resource, but its affects are discussed in later chapters in the context of competition.

Conditions are similar to resources in that they can change, effect growth and elicit differential species responses. However, conditions are not consumed in the sense resources are. In this book temperature and some properties of soil, such as pH, are described as conditions. The reader should be wary of any clear-cut boundaries between resources and conditions. Human intervention also muddies the boundaries between conditions and resources.

The second portion of this book covers population dynamics, species competition and disturbances. Population dynamics cover species growth and how cultural practices may impact growth. Species competition including intraspecific (within the same species), and interspecific (between species), are covered in separate chapters. Disturbances which affect the competitiveness of species centers on the effects of mowing and predators (pests).

As you read this book, it is my hope that you will come to see turfgrass management as more than a technical manager, but through the eyes of a turfgrass ecologist.

1

Climate, Weather and Turfgrasses

*Everyone talks about the weather, but nobody
does anything about it. — Mark Twain, writer*

THE PLANET EARTH is composed of the lithosphere, hydrosphere and atmosphere. The lithosphere is the solid phase of the Earth including the crust. The hydrosphere is the total amount of liquid and frozen water on or near the Earth's surface. Oceans, polar ice caps, ponds and groundwater are chief components of the hydrosphere. The atmosphere is the region of gases and water vapors that envelop the Earth and are held there by gravity.

The living component, known as the biosphere, is the entire realm where all organisms live. The biosphere includes small fractions each of the lithosphere, hydrosphere and atmosphere. Ecosystems within the biosphere range from the vast, such as tropical rain forests, to those that contain turfgrasses. All of the ecosystems, except for a few in the deepest parts of the oceans, are influenced by global weather patterns.

Climate and weather define the environmental parameters for turfgrass adaptation and survival. Both climate and weather are similar in that they involve atmospheric variables, but differ in their duration. Weather is the total effect of atmospheric variables at a given place for a brief period of time. Climate represents a composite of daily weather conditions for a given area over a longer period of time.

The primary elements used to describe climate and weather are solar energy; temperature; moisture, including precipitation and humidity; winds; and atmospheric pressure. These factors vary in their amount, distribution and intensity, and cause weather to vary daily and climate to vary among regions.

SOLAR RADIATION

The Earth intercepts only about one- to two-billionths of the sun's total energy output. Most of the sun's solar energy intercepted by the Earth is reflected back into space by clouds and air particles or absorbed by clouds, dust and water vapor. The solar energy that does reach the Earth's surface causes a differential heating.

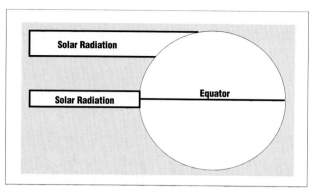

Figure 1. Light rays are more concentrated in the equatorial region than the polar regions. This causes unequal heating resulting in air movement northward and southward from the equator.

Incoming rays from the sun are more direct at the equator resulting in greater heating, while rays hitting at higher latitudes are more dispersed resulting in lesser heating. (Figure 1) Uneven solar heating of the globe causes initial global air movement to occur both northward and southward from the equator.

As the heated air moves away from the equator, disruptions to the flow occur because of the Earth's rotation and land masses. The Earth rotates from east to west with the fastest rotation occurring at the equator and the slowest at the poles. The rotational forces of the Earth, along with the differential speed at which it turns, produces easterly and westerly movement of the air masses.

Land surfaces will heat and cool more rapidly than large bodies of water. The moderating effect of water is due to its high specific heat (energy required to raise/lower temperatures), and depth which allows for diffusion and distribution of solar energy. Differential heating created by land masses and large bodies of water cause changes in atmospheric pressure. Atmospheric pressure decreases when warm air

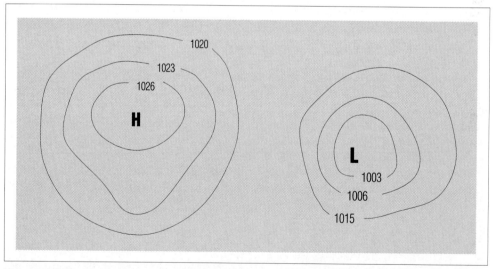

Figure 2. High and low pressure centers are defined on weather maps by changes in pressure. Pressure units are millibars reduced to sea level. Many of the wind arrows are inferred from isobars. (From Strahler, A.N. and A.H. Strahler. 1984. Elements of Physical Geography. John Wiley and Sons.)

rises and increases when cold air sinks. Pressure differences occurring around the world result in winds which are responsible for disrupting the northward or southward air movement from the equator. The interaction of warm and cold air causes storms. The circulation of air around these storms is important in transporting heat poleward to compensate for radiation deficiencies in higher latitudes.

The planet Earth is composed of the lithosphere, hydrosphere and atmosphere. (Courtesy of NASA)

Air moves both vertically and horizontally. Vertical air movement is commonly associated with thunderstorms as updrafts and downdrafts. Horizontal movement is termed wind and its speed is substantially greater than vertical movement. Air moves in a horizontal direction in response to changes in barometric pressure from high pressure areas to low pressure areas. These pressure changes across the surface of a weather map constitute pressure gradients. When a pressure gradient exists, air molecules drift in the same direction. For example, a sea breeze forms from the rapid heating of air over the land which decreases pressure. At the same time, the pressure remains high over the water. This sets up a pressure gradient from high (over water) to low (over land) with the result in air movement from the ocean to land.

Changes in barometric pressure are delineated on a weather map by isobars (lines connecting places with the same atmospheric pressure) which identify pressure centers. (Figure 2) A low pressure area (low), often called a cyclone, is an area having a lower pressure than the surrounding areas. An area of low pressure without an identifiable center is termed a trough. Winds associated with a low pressure system flow in a counterclockwise fashion in the Northern Hemisphere. Low pressure systems move rapidly bringing cloudy weather with rain or snow. Low pressure systems with severe storms are more accurately termed hurricanes, typhoons, tornadoes or tropical storms.

A high pressure system with increasing pressure toward a given center is termed an anticyclone. Winds flow in a clockwise manner around a high pressure area in the Northern Hemisphere. If an elongated area of high pressure is found without an identifiable center it is termed a ridge. High pressure sys-

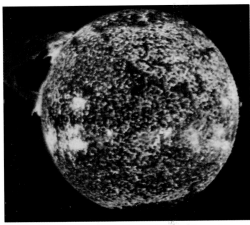

Weather results from differential heating of the air by our source of solar radiation, the sun. (Courtesy of NASA)

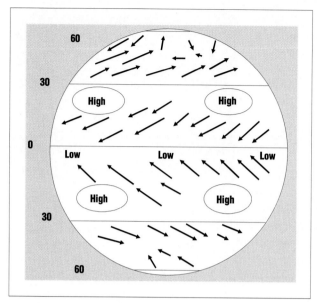

Figure 3. Schematic of the global surface winds disregarding the disruptive affects of land masses.

tems usually bring fair weather, clear skies, less wind and become relatively stationary compared to lows. Although anticyclones are not associated with moisture, they do play an important role in weather.

Summer heat waves occur when high pressure areas become stationary over the Southeastern United States. The clockwise flow brings warm air north from the tropics. In the winter, high pressure areas form over the arctic bringing cold air to the United States.

WINDS

As previously mentioned, winds develop from changes in barometric pressure. The major global patterns of surface winds are shown in Figure 3. Trade winds both in the Northern Hemisphere and Southern Hemisphere flow from a subtropical high pressure area toward the equatorial low pressure trough. Trade winds are of little interest to turfgrass managers. However, the winds that move from the western sides of the subtropical highs into the latitude region of 35 degrees to 60 degrees north and south, termed westerlies, are important. Rapidly moving cyclonic storms are common in this wind belt. In addition, a narrow band of strong winds called the jet stream exists within the zone of westerly winds. Jet streams are important because cyclones form beneath the stream and initially track along the same path as the jet stream.

Besides global wind patterns, local winds may develop that result in regional environmental conditions stressful to turfgrasses. In Southern California, for instance, a local condition called the Santa Ana winds occurs causing a hot dry wind flow. The Santa Ana winds develop from a strong anticyclone center in the desert regions of Southern California that blow through narrow mountain gaps, intensifying as they head toward the Pacific Ocean. Santa Ana winds bring very dry conditions which can cause high evapotranspiration losses from turfgrass stands.

Chinook winds are produced by locally strong winds passing over a mountain range. Chinook winds are common to coastal regions of Washington and Oregon bringing warm, moist air in a southwesterly direction. As the wind passes and descends on the lee side of the mountain, the air is heated and dried. Chinook winds bring drying conditions that may cause high evapotranspiration losses from turfgrass stands.

Monsoon winds, to a large extent, influence weather patterns in Southeast Asia.

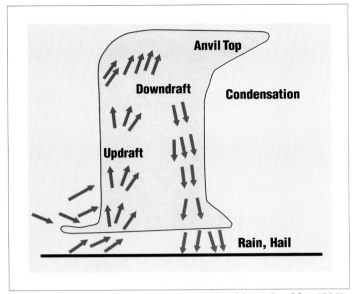

Figure 4. A thunderstorm cross section. (Strahler & Strahler, 1984)

In the summer, a cyclone develops with an associated strong flow of air. Moving from the higher pressure areas of the Indian Ocean and the southwestern Pacific, warm humid air moves northward toward the cyclone into India, Indochina, China and Japan. The result is an extended period of heavy rainfall called a monsoon. In the winter, a strong high pressure area dominates the Southwest Asia land mass producing a strong outward flow of air toward the Pacific and Indian oceans. The winter monsoon brings months of dry weather to Southeast Asia.

Wind impacts turfgrass management in various ways. In addition to increasing evapotranspiration, wind can enhance the spread of weed seeds and, in sparsely covered turf areas, increase soil erosion. Moderate levels of wind, on the other hand, promote the consumption of carbon dioxide by photosynthesis and on occasion prevents frost by disrupting a temperature inversion.

PRECIPITATION

Precipitation in the form of rain or snow is critical to the growth and development of turfgrass plants. In Chapter 4, the role of water in turfgrass survival is discussed. However, precipitation in the form of severe storms such as thunderstorms, hail and hurricanes may cause locally stressful conditions for plant growth.

Precipitation occurs when a large air mass rises and the air is cooled below the dew point. Dew point is the critical temperature at which air becomes saturated during cooling. Below the dew point, condensation usually occurs. As the air mass rises, the temperature drops creating an adiabatic process.

The drop in temperature is often in the range of 5.5 degrees Fahrenheit per 1,000 square feet of increased elevation. The combination of moist air converging to an area of low barometric pressure and the subsequent drop in temperature from the adiabatic process results in the formation of clouds and the production of precipitation.

THUNDERSTORMS

A thunderstorm is an intense local storm that produces heavy precipitation, lightning and thunder in a relatively short period of time. During the summer, thunderstorms develop from a spontaneous rise in air. This mechanism of rapid, upward air movement is known as convection. Convection is a series of strong updrafts of air. As the convective air rises, it is cooled adiabatically below the dew point leading to condensation. At this point, the rising air column appears as a cloud (cumulus). Although condensation is occurring, the top of the cloud continues to rise higher into the atmosphere. Spontaneously rising

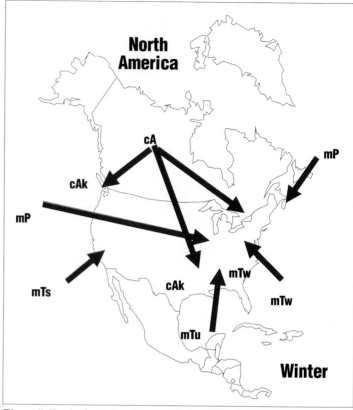

Figure 5. Typical winter air mass flow in North America.

air during condensation is described as unstable. Unstable air undergoing the convection process gives rise to heavy precipitation. (Figure 4) Unstable air is most likely to be found in warm, humid areas.

Hailstones may be produced in thunderstorms when water is rapidly cooled to ice pellets and suspended in strong updrafts. After hailstones grow to a diameter of 1 to 2 inches, they escape the updraft and fall to the Earth. Hailstones may cause severe physical damage to turfgrasses. For example, if hailstones fall on a golf course, sunken holes develop disrupting the playability of the turf.

TROPICAL CYCLONES

In some instances, cyclones of great intensity develop over oceans in tropical regions. These tropical cyclones are known by various names such as hurricanes in the Atlantic Ocean, typhoons in the Western Pacific and cyclones in the Indian Ocean and Australia. Tropical cyclones may cause tremendous damage to land areas that lie in the path of these storms. Hurricanes have wreaked havoc during the late summer months in turf areas along the East Coast of the United States. Heavy rain, flooding and high wave action are associated with hurricanes. High wave action

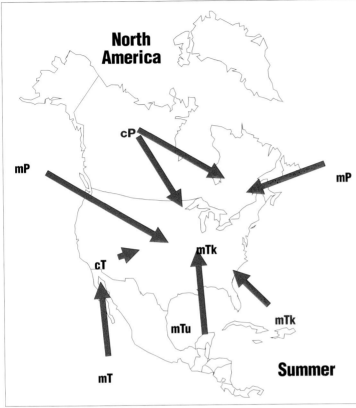

Figure 6. Typical summer air mass flow in North America.

along coastal areas may result in the deposition of salt on the turf causing plant stress.

AIR MASSES

Forecasting weather mainly involves recognizing various air masses. Cyclones of middle and high latitudes depend on the coming together of large bodies of air of different physical properties. A body of air that remains over an extensive, homogeneous surface for a period of time, acquiring the characteristics of that region, is known as an air mass. The area where air mass takes on land or water surface characteristics is called a source region. An air mass that develops over a source region is relatively uniform regarding temperature and moisture. Based on temperature and moisture characteristics, air masses are categorized as arctic/antarctic (A), polar (P) and tropical (T). These air masses are further divided depending on whether they developed over an ocean or a large land area. If an air mass develops over an ocean it is given the designation "m" for maritime, and if over land a "c" for continental. An additional term used to describe an air mass is whether it is warmer (w) than the underlying surface or colder (k) than the underlying surface. An example of an air mass designation is cAk which represents a continental arctic cold air mass. (Table 1) Common winter and summer air mass patterns for North America are shown in figures 5 and 6.

FRONTS

Once an air mass leaves its source region, a prescribed path is followed. As two different air masses converge, a weather change occurs. Air masses do not freely mix, thus a boundary — termed a front — develops between the two air masses. Three major types of fronts may occur: cold, warm and occluded. (Figure 7) A cold front is a line along which a wedge of cold air is underrunning and displacing a warm air mass. Cold fronts are generally accompanied by temperature and humidity decreases, pressure increases and, in North America, a wind shift from the southwest to northwest leading to precipitation.

The weather along a cold front varies depending on how fast the front is moving. A slow-moving cold front is characterized by a general upward movement of warm air along the frontal boundary. The cloud cover and precipitation is extensive with showers and thunderstorms at and immediately to the rear of the front. A fast-moving cold front causes the warm air near the surface to be pushed rapidly upward while high level warm air is descending along the front. Generally speaking this type of front brings a relatively narrow band,

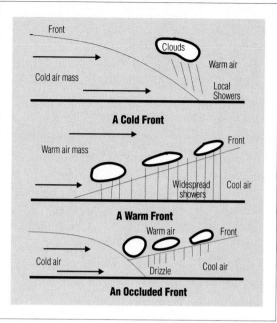

Figure 7. Three major types of fronts are illustrated above in conjunction with their associated moisture patterns. (See text for description.)

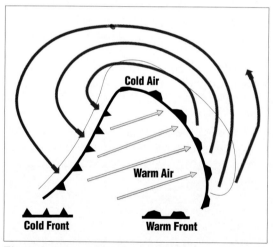

Figure 8. An example of a wave cyclone as it might appear on a weather map. Extensive precipitation is occurring along the warm front with a clearing behind it. As the cold front moves through a narrow range, intensive precipitation occurs.

but very intensive thunderstorms with rapid clearing as the front passes through.

A warm front is a line between an advancing warm air mass and a retreating colder mass of air. General characteristics of a warm front are a shift in the wind from the southeast to southwest or west, temperatures are warmer behind the front and precipitation can extend up to 300 miles in front of the warm front.

An occluded front occurs when warm and cold air mix. As the air masses intermix, the warm air is forced upward while the cold air remains along the ground. This front is generally characterized by low cloud ceiling and rainfall may be a shower or drizzle.

WAVE CYCLONES

A common weather disturbance in middle to high latitudes stems from wave cyclones. As a cold and warm air mass converge, each air mass invades the territory of the other. In the northern hemisphere, the cold air mass turns in a southerly direction while the warm air turns in a northerly direction. This produces a vortex-looking cyclone on the weather map. As the warm air turns, a portion of the cold air moves behind the warm air pro-

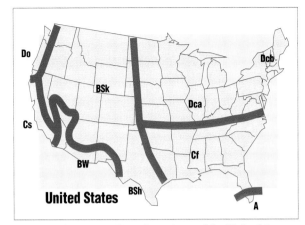

Figure 9. The major climatic regions of the United States.

ducing a wave of weather activity. A wave cyclone is shown on the weather map in Figure 8. General weather patterns associated with a wave cyclone are (Neiburger et al, 1982):

1. A thickening cloud sheet approaching from the west as the barometric pressure begins to fall slowly, but steadily.
2. As the warm front approaches, light rain occurs and gets heavier as the front gets closer.
3. With the passage of the warm front, winds shift southwesterly, temperatures rise and the sky clears.
4. As the cold front approaches, a rapid pressure drop occurs.
5. The arrival of the cold front brings northwest winds, a rapid decrease in temperature, a rise in pressure and showers or thunderstorms of great intensity, but of short duration.

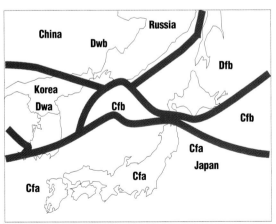

Figure 10. The major regions of Japan, Korea, China and Russia.

Wave cyclones move in an eastward direction with deviations occurring in a northward or southward course.

Turf management decisions such as irrigation frequency and disease control applications may be based on fronts and wave cyclones. For instance, a wave cyclone initially brings moisture and warm temperatures; conditions favorable for warm weather diseases. However, depending on how fast the cold front approaches with a subsequent decrease in temperature, disease control measures may not be needed since conditions favorable for warm weather disease development have changed.

CLIMATE

Climate defines the regions of adaptation of cool- and warm-season turfgrasses. Cool-season turfgrasses are adapted to areas of moderate temperature with precipitation and temperature defining the limits of their survival. Warm-season grasses are adapted to high temperature regions with limits to adaptation defined by a lack of cold tolerance.

Classification maps are used to delineate world climatic regions based on the interaction of air masses. Various classification systems exist including those based on air masses. The system most widely used is based on the work by Koppen and is described by Trewartha and Horn (1980) who break down the Earth's climatic regions as:

A. Tropical: Frost limit in continental locations; in marine areas 65 F (average temperature) for the coolest month

B. Dry: Precipitation limited; where potential evaporation equals precipitation

C. Subtropical: Eight months where the average monthly temperature is 50 F or above

D. Temperate: Four months where the average monthly temperature is 50 F or above

E. Boreal: 1 (warmest) month 50 F (average monthly temperature) or above

F. Polar: All months below 50 F (average monthly temperature)

Within these climatic groups are types of climate. Climates are generally based on precipitation. Listed below are the abbreviations and descriptions of the major groups and types of climate. Temperatures represent the average monthly temperature. For the United States, the major groups of climate are A,B,C and D. (Table 2 and Figure 9)

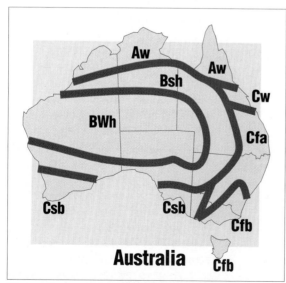

Figure 11. The climatic regions of Australia.

A. *Tropical:*
r (rainy) = 10 to 12 months wet; 0 to 2 months dry
w = winter (low-sun period) dry; more than 2 months dry
s = summer (high-sun period) dry; rare in A climates

B. *Dry:*
h = hot; 8 months or more with average temperature over 50 F
k = cold; fewer than 8 months average temperature above

50 degrees F
    s = summer dry
    w = winter dry
C and D. *Subtropical and Temperate:*
    a = hot summer; warmest month over 72 F
    b = cool summer; warmest month below 72 F
    c = continental; cold month under 32 F
    f = no dry season; difference between dri-
    est and wettest month less than required
    for s and w; driest month of summer more
    than 1.2 inches

A view of a hurricane from space. (Courtesy of NASA)

    o = oceanic or marine; cold month over 32 F
    s = summer dry; at least 3 times as much
    rain in winter half year as in summer half
    year; driest summer month less than 1.2 inches; annual total under 35
    inches.
    w = winter dry; at least 10 times as much rain in summer half year as in winter
    half year
F. *all months below 50 F*
    t = tundra; warmest month between 32 F and 50 F
    i = ice cap; all months below 32 F
It would be provincial to think that the only important climatic regions occur in the
United States. In Great Britain and most of Europe, the climate is classified as Cfb

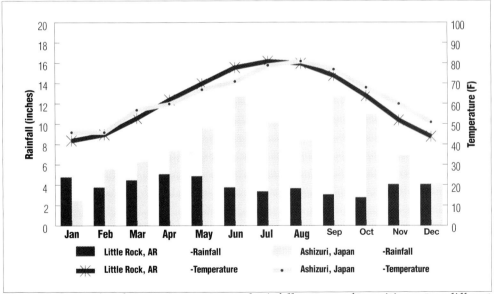

Figure 12. Comparison between temperature and rainfall patterns of two cities on two different continents that have the same regional classification.

(cool summers and no dry seasons). Along the Mediterranean Sea the climate changes to hotter summers and drier periods (Csa). Japan and Australia, on the other hand, have variable zones of climatic adaptation. (Figures 10 and 11)

In classifying zones of adaptation, variation can exist within regions. Turfgrass managers must be careful to study other important factors, in addition to a broad descriptive map, when determining climatic conditions. For

Hailstones as large as golf balls may result from intensive thunderstorms. (Courtesy of Scott Hurt)

example, Little Rock, Ark., and Ashizuri, Japan, are located at approximately the same latitude (34° N and 32° N, respectively), roughly at the same height above sea level (357 and 213 feet), the same climatic region (Cfa) and roughly have the same monthly mean temperatures. (Figure 12) Yet, the requirements for growing turfgrass are considerably different.

In Ashizuri, the amount of rainfall during the summer is considerably greater than Little Rock. This is a result of the Asian Monsoons which may hit Japan during the summer bringing extremely high rainfall to some parts of the country. In this situation, practices such as mowing, fertilization, topdressing and pesticide applications become more difficult to execute because of the amount of rainfall.

Attempts have been made within the United States to grow turfgrasses in climatic regions outside of their adaptation. Serious consideration must be given to the climatic type before a turfgrass is introduced. For example, creeping bentgrass which is adapted to the East and Midwest has been introduced into Florida. A case can be made that the temperatures and humidity during Florida summers are not much higher than found in Cincinnati, Ohio, at certain times. However, the duration of high temperatures and humidity is considerably longer in Florida as the climatic type indicates. This makes maintaining creeping bentgrass both expensive and tenuous.

In comparison, growing creeping bentgrass in the climatic group B (e.g., Arizona) has been successful due to the low humidity in the region. However, with water scarcity a current and future concern in the region, the selection of creeping bentgrass for use should be carefully weighed.

Difficulty arises in managing turfgrasses at points where boarders of climatic regions overlap. An example is where the climatic regions Dca and Cf are in contact. (Figure 9) It is important to note that this line represents the norm based on a 30-year average. However, from year to year this line will adjust upward or downward given the local weather. The area that is defined by the line between Dca and Cf is often referred to as the transition zone. Metropolitan areas such as Washington-Baltimore, Cincinnati, Louisville, St. Louis and Kansas City fall within the transition zone.

What makes the transition zone such a difficult area to grow turf is that it is too hot and humid during the summer for most cool-season turfgrasses and too cold during the winter for warm-season turfgrasses. A wide range of grasses such as tall fescue, zoysiagrass, creeping bentgrass, perennial ryegrass and bermudagrass are grown in the transition zone with varying degrees of success.

In summary, solar energy, the rotation of the Earth and land masses interact to impart the weather and climatic conditions that determine turfgrass adaptation. In this chapter, the effects of solar radiation and precipitation have been discussed on a global scale. In the following chapters, solar radiation and precipitation effects on turfgrass growth will be discussed.

North American Air Masses And Where They Originate

Air Mass	Temperature	Source Region
Maritime tropical (mT)	72 to 86F	Tropical and subtropical oceans, Amazon rainforests and Congo basin. Forms over stagnant high pressure areas. The air is warm due to the low latitude, and is able to hold considerable moisture.
Continental Tropical (cT)	86 to 108F	Subtropical deserts (Sahara, Australia). The air over these land masses is hot and dry.
Maritime Polar (mP)	32 to 57F	Oceans, toward the pole, latitude 45 to 50 degrees. These types of air masses are generally moist.
Continental Arctic (cA)	-67 to -31F	Antarctica, Greenland, northern Europe and Asia, north of 55 degrees latitude. During the summer continental polar is used for air masses formed over the arctic and during the winter for air developed over the snow areas. The air is characterized by being dry, very cold and stable in lower latitudes.
Continental Polar (cP), su	41 to 59F	Northern portions of North America and Eurasia. Air moves across the Great Lakes cooling and stabilizing temperatures and resulting in nice weather.

TABLE 1.   *(Source: Trewartha and Horn, 1980)*

Major Climatic Regions of the United States and the Adaptation of Turfgrasses

Climatic Region	Description*	Some Adapted Turfgrasses
Dcb	Temperate region with 4 to 7 months inclusive over 50 F with cool summers (warmest month below 72F) and continental weather during the winter with a cold month under 32 F.	bluegrass, bentgrass, ryegrass (marginal), fine fescue
Dca	Temperate region with 4 to 7 months inclusive over 50 F with continental climate having a cold month under 32 F. Summer months are hot with warmest month over 72 F.	bluegrass, ryegrass, tall fescue, bentgrass, fine fescue
Cf	8 to 12 months over 50 F with the coolest month below 65 F. No dry season; driest month of summer more than 1.2 inches.	bermudagrass, zoysiagrass, tall fescue (northern), bluegrass (northern), bentgrass (northern), ryegrass, St. Augustinegrass (coastal)
Aw	Killing frost absent; in marine areas cold month above 65 F. The winter is dry, with more than 2 months dry.	bermudagrass, St. Augustinegrass
BSk	Region where the potential evaporation rate exceeds the precipitation rate, summers are dry and relatively cold with fewer than 8 months above 50 F.	buffalograss, bluegrass, tall fescue, fine fescue, ryegrass, bentgrass
Bsh	Similar to BSk except the summers are hot with 8 months or more above 50 F.	bermudagrass, zoysiagrass, buffalograss, tall fescue, bluegrass, bentgrass
BW	Regions where potential evaporation rate exceeds the precipitation rate in a desert or arid condition.	bermudagrass, zoysiagrass, buffalograss, tall fescue, bentgrass
Cs	Region where 8 to 12 months over 50 F with coolest month below 65 F. Summers are dry at least 3 times as much in the winter as in the summer.	bluegrass, bermudagrass, zoysiagrass, bentgrass, ryegrass
Do	Region where 4 to 7 months inclusive over 50 F. Climate is oceanic, cold month over 32 F.	bluegrass, ryegrass

TABLE 2.
* temperatures are monthly average

(Source: Trewartha and Horn, 1980.)

2

Light, as a Resource

We all know what light is, but it is not easy to tell what it is. — Samuel Johnson, writer

THE CAPTURE OF ENERGY is the fundamental base upon which all life depends. During photosynthesis, plants capture the sun's energy, store it in organic compounds and draw on it as needed for growth, reproduction and survival. The sun provides abundant energy; and while its light does not appear to be a limiting factor for growth, changes in quantity and quality — brought about by competition between turfgrass species and surrounding plant material — results in light becoming a limiting resource.

LIGHT

Solar radiation consists of a broad spectrum of wavelengths from very short (cosmic rays) to very long (radio waves). Light which is visible to the human eye is a narrow portion of the radiation spectrum ranging from 380 to 775 nanometers (nm). (Figure 1) Within the visible range are the violet, blue, green, yellow, orange and red wavelengths. The visible range is the photosynthetically active radiation. Wavelengths shorter than 380 nm consist of ultraviolet, X-rays, gamma rays and cosmic rays while those greater than 775 nm include infrared and radio waves.

Wavelengths shorter than 380 nm are ionizing and may cause mutation or detrimental morphological effects. This is a result of high energy within these wavelengths that can break bonds in organic molecules. Turfgrass breeders have used shortwave radiation (gamma rays) to induce mutations in vegetatively propagated turfgrasses for the purpose of adding genetic variation. (Powell, et al, 1974) Under natural exposure, the plant's cuticle helps protect internal leaf functions by filtering ultraviolet light. At the opposite end of the spectrum, infrared wavelengths are not energetic enough to power chemical changes. Thus, the absorption of longer wavelengths such as infrared only increases plant temperature.

Plants either absorb, reflect or transmit light depending on the wavelength.

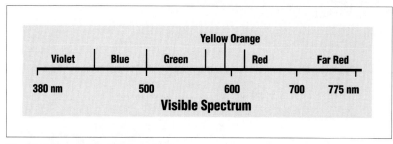

Figure 1. The visible light spectrum.

Absorption of photosynthetically active radiation is determined by the chloroplast pigments (primarily green and blue). Approximately 70 percent of the photosynthetically usable radiation that enters the mesophyll is absorbed. Leaves reflect 70 percent of radiation from infrared regions, but only 6 percent to 12 percent in the photosynthetically active region. As a rule, very little is reflected in the ultraviolet region.

Green light is strongly reflected (the reason why plants appear green to the eye) as are orange, yellow and red, to a smaller degree. Transmission is greatest in the green and far-red spectral regions, but varies with leaf thickness. Thin leaves transmit more light than thick leaves.

A practical application of light in turf is the use of infrared photography. Infrared photography, which measures the invisible radiation beyond 700 nm, has been used to measure both abiotic and biotic stresses on turf. On infrared film, turfgrass that is green appears pink while brown grass appears blue-green. Stressed turfgrass exhibiting injury from pathogens, insects, lack of moisture, freezing, low-light conditions and traffic lose infrared reflectance before visible changes in the plant occur. Thus, a plant may appear healthy to the human eye, but infrared photography may reveal internal plant problems. Infrared photography has been mentioned as a helpful tool in integrated pest management programs for monitoring problem spots before visible symptoms appear. (McCarty et al, 1990)

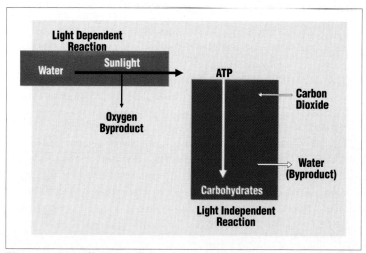

Figure 2. Overall view of the photosynthetic reaction. In the light dependent reaction, the combination of light and water produces ATP which is then used in the light independent reaction to produce energy storage compounds.

ENERGY CAPTURING AND RELEASING DEVICES:

Photosynthesis:
Light absorption

by plants occurs in chloroplasts where it is later converted into usable energy through photosynthesis. The overall photosynthetic reaction is simply expressed as:

$$Energy + 24\,H_2O + 12\,CO_2 \longrightarrow 12\,O_2 + C_{12}H_{24}O_{12} + 12H_2O$$

This equation may be broken down into two distinct groups of reactions. (Figure 2) The first reaction group is light dependent and captures light energy storing it in energy-rich bonds of adenosine triphosphate (ATP). Electrons, hydrogen and oxygen are released when water is split in the light dependent reactions. The oxygen released by plants is a byproduct of this reaction. The hydrogen and electrons help form ATP. Light independent reactions shape the second group, also called the dark reactions, taking the energy (ATP) from the light dependent reactions and reducing CO_2 to sucrose. (Figures 2 and 3) Sucrose molecules are transported or linked into carbohydrate chains called starches and cellulose. The light independent reactions are cyclic allowing continual formation of sucrose.

Respiration: At some point, sugars and starches (carbohydrates) break down

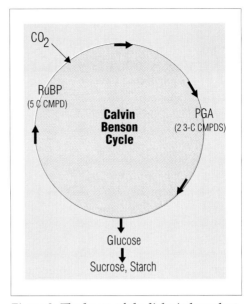

Figure 3. The heart of the light independent reaction is the Calvin-Benson cycle. In the Calvin-Benson cycle, carbon dioxide is first attached to ribulose bisphosphate (RuBP) forming a 6-carbon compound which is quickly broken down into two 3-carbon compounds [phosphglycerate (PGA)]. Next, the PGA receives phosphate group from the ATP formed in the light dependent reaction. Some of these compounds (phosphoglyceraldehyde) go on and form simple sugars (through additional light independent reactions) while others undergo rearrangement to form new RuBP.

The capture of the sun's energy by photosynthesis is the basic process that all life is based on.

to provide energy and metabolites for cellular growth and maintenance. Energy release is termed respiration, a process which involves two pathways called aerobic and anaerobic. Aerobic respiration uses oxygen as a final electronic acceptor while in anaerobic respiration, something besides oxygen is used as an acceptor. Anaerobic respiration for this discussion is of minor importance and is primarily used by sulphur reducing bacteria and, in some instances if oxygen is absent, denitrifying bacteria. Glycolysis is the first energy releasing pathway in aerobic respiration (also in anaerobic respiration). Glycolysis occurs in the cytoplasm of the cell and initially breaks down sugars. The energy releasing efficiency of glycolysis is low compared to the remaining aerobic energy releasing pathways.

Within the mitocondria of the cell, the aerobic pathways — Krebs cycle and the electron transport — are found. The Krebs cycle and electron transport release the greatest amount of energy (ATP). Complete aerobic respiration of a molecule of sucrose yields up to 76 ATPs. At the end of the last group of reactions — electron transport — oxygen acts as the final electron acceptor of "spent" electrons with water and CO_2 being the final byproducts. (Figure 4)

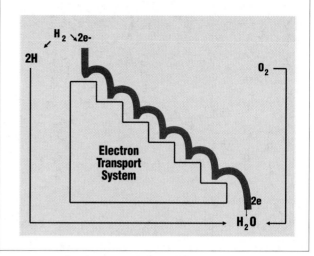

Figure 4. As electrons move down the electron transport system, ATP is released and used for metabolic processes. In the final step, oxygen serves as an electron acceptor with the final byproduct being water.

$$Energy + 24\ H_2O + 12\ CO_2 \xrightarrow[respiration]{photosynthesis} 12\ O_2 + C_{12}H_{24}O_{12} + 12H_2O$$

Turf managers, through their cultural and chemical practices, directly affect photosynthesis and respiration. For example, the presence of oxygen is needed for root respiration which is important in the active process of water absorption. If oxygen is absent, due to a compacted or waterlogged soil, water uptake is restricted causing the plant to wilt. This phenomenon is termed wet wilt.

In addition, the use of plant growth regulators on turf may induce unexpected plant responses. For example, the application of a gibberellin synthesis inhibiting plant growth regulator may cause the turf to become darker green. The dark green response is caused by interfering in respiration reactions. The molecule that is accountable for the darker green color is acetyl coenzyme A (CoA) which is involved in the Krebs cycle. When gibberellic synthesis is inhibited, CoA is diverted to other reaction pathways such as chlorophyll production which results in a greener plant.

Turfgrass plants that have high net photosynthetic activity (photosynthesis > respiration) form turfs having better quality, and are more likely to be tolerant of environmental stresses. (Watschke et al, 1972; Mehall et al, 1984) In 1972, Watschke et al. found that Kentucky bluegrass cultivars with high net photosynthetic activity

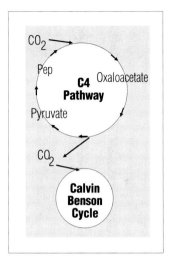

Figure 5. In C4 plants carbon dioxide is fixed preceding the Calvin-Benson cycle. In this reaction, carbon dioxide is attached to phosphoenol pyruvate (PEP), forming oxaloacetate (4-carbon compound, thus the name C4 plants) which is transferred deeper into the leaf with the carbon being released and fixed again in the Calvin-Benson cycle.

better tolerated high temperature stress. Practices such as raising mowing heights, reducing frequency of mowing and minimizing nitrogen can increase leaf area, thus increasing the potential photosynthetic rate during high temperature stress.

CO_2: CARBON SOURCE

Carbon is an essential component of all organic molecules. The source of carbon is carbon dioxide (CO_2) which enters the photosynthetic process during the light independent reaction. (Figure 2)

Carbon dioxide is attached to a 5-carbon sugar (ribulose bisphosphate) which quickly breaks down to two 3-carbon compounds. The 3-carbon compounds ultimately contribute to sucrose formation. Plants that fix carbon according to this process are termed C3 plants. Some plants have a mechanism of fixing CO_2 preceding the light independent reaction via a 4-carbon compound. This allows for the cycling of CO_2 deeper into the leaf blade before being released for use in the light independent reaction. Plants that can fix CO_2 before it entering the light independent reaction are referred to as C4 plants. (Figure 5)

Photorespiration, not to be confused with respiration, is the wasteful use of carbon (i.e., CO_2). Photorespiration occurs when oxygen levels in the plant increase in relation to the carbon dioxide. High oxygen levels can occur when stomates (tiny openings in the leaf)

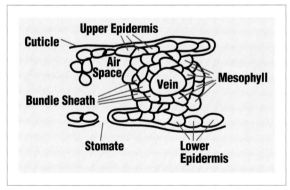

Figure 6. Cross section of a turfgrass leaf. In C4 plants, carbon dioxide is cycled deeper into the bundle sheaths compared to C3 plants before being released. This mechanism contributes to the low photorespiration rates of C3 plants.

close, causing a reduction in CO_2 exchange. Oxygen competes with CO_2 for uptake in the light independent reactions. Conditions favorable for photorespiration are hot, dry days. Under these conditions, the plant leaf will close stomates cutting off transpiration. This results in oxygen buildup in the leaf which then competes with CO_2 for uptake by ribulose bisphosphate. The end result is a 50 percent reduction in carbon fixation.

Plants vary in their rates of photorespiration. Under hot, dry con-

29

ditions C3 plants have high rates of photorespiration while C4 plants have little if any photorespiration. As previously mentioned, stomates close under dry conditions which can lead to increasing amounts of internal plant oxygen levels. However, a C4 plant is able to concentrate CO_2 deeper into the leaf for use in photosynthesis. (Figure 6) A C3 plant is unable to do this. The efficiency of C4 plants for obtaining CO_2 can be demonstrated with increasing light intensity. With C3 plants, increasing levels of light increase the fixation of CO_2 until the light level reaches 1/2 of the full sun. As light levels increase beyond this point, CO_2 fixation does not increase and will

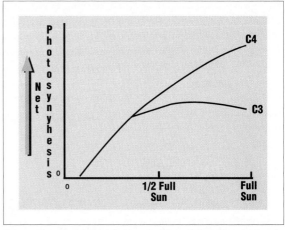

Figure 7. Comparison between C3 and C4 plants regarding net photosynthesis. With increasing light intensity C4 plants continue to photosynthesize at an accelerated rate. C3 plants increase net photosynthesis with increasing light to a point (1/2 full sun). Beyond this position, the ability to fix increasing CO_2 levels off and decreases (photorespiration).

actually decrease (result of photorespiration). However, C4 plants are able to continue to fix CO_2 with increasing light levels. (Figure 7)

From a competitive standpoint, during warm summer months, C4 plants have a tremendous advantage over C3 plants due to their ability to photosynthesize at higher temperatures without losing energy through photorespiration. Cool-season grasses (C3) at high temperatures fix carbon at half the rate of warm-season grasses (C4) resulting in reduced growth and less competition. This is a major reason why crabgrass, a C4 plant is so competitive with Kentucky bluegrass, a C3 plant, during hot dry summers.

The darker green color of the turfgrass is in response to a plant growth regulator that is a gibberellic inhibitor.

PHOTOPERIOD

The number of hours of daylight in relation to hours of darkness is termed photoperiod. Photoperiod influences the growth of various turf species differently. For example, bermudagrass grows most rapidly when solar radiation is greater than 13 hours. However, during periods of shorter day lengths such as in the fall, bermudagrass growth slows naturally regardless of whether irrigation or fertilizer has been applied. (Burton et al, 1988) The opposite effect occurs with some cool-season turfgrasses. Perennial ryegrass and annual bluegrass have their greatest tillering rates in spring and fall during shorter day-length periods. Some turfgrasses such as Kentucky bluegrass have a constant tillering rate regardless of day length. (Brede and Duich, 1986)

Changes in growth patterns occur in response to photoperiod. Cool-season turfgrasses, such as creeping bentgrass, change their growth habits in response to day length. In the spring and fall, creeping bentgrass grows quite prostrate, but when day length increases, growth becomes more upright. The impact on management practices is to groom, vertical mow and brush during the spring and fall to try to make the bentgrass more upright. During the summer, when creeping bentgrass is more upright, these practices are needed less frequently.

Photoperiod also influences when turfgrass plants will flower and are classified as:

Long-day plants — triggered to flower when a critical day length is exceeded. Vegetative growth occurs when the critical day length is not met.

Short-day plants — flower only when the day length is shorter than some critical period. When the day length is exceeded, vegetative growth occurs.

Day-neutral plants — do not respond to photoperiod and may flower under any light condition. Long-day plants will flower in spring in response to longer days while short-day plants flower in the autumn. Day-neutral plants flower as soon as they are mature, and not in response to daylength.

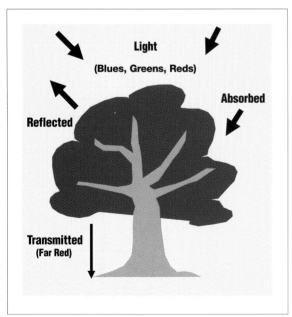

Figure 8. Various fates and changes in light as it comes into contact with a tree.

Most turfgrass species, with the exception of bermudagrass and Canadian bluegrass, have a short-day photoperiod for optimum flower induction. However, seed-head development may occur with a different photoperiod. For example, Kentucky bluegrass flower induction is optimum during short-day lengths, but flower development is greatest during long-day periods. Turf managers may observe certain Kentucky bluegrass turfs (cultivar dependent) producing seedheads in the late spring or early summer. Most cool-season turfgrasses produce seed under long-days. However, some cool-season turfgrasses produce seedheads over a wide range of photoperiods. Annual bluegrass and perennial ryegrass flower over a wide range of photoperiods. Fortunately, most turfgrass species do not produce seedheads under normal turfgrass management practices.

A light-sensitive pigment molecule known as phytochrome is involved in flowering and seed germination. Phytochrome detects light breaks during the night which can inhibit flowering in short-day plants and promote flowering in long-day plants. Extended day lengths activate phytochrome for a longer period of time. Thus, long-day

Shade may result in a change in the quality and quantity of light intercepted by the turf and affect its growth. (Courtesy of John Street)

plants may flower more rapidly and produce more flowers than short-day plants.

Phytochrome exists in two forms, P_r and P_{fr}. The P_r form is an inactive state while the P_{fr} form is the active state that promotes hormonal activity necessary for seed germination and plant growth. The P_{fr} form is activated in the presence of light. When enough P_{fr} accumulates in a seed, germination occurs. (McDonald et al, 1992) Prolonged darkness and/or increased temperatures generally causes P_{fr} to revert to P_r. In dry seeds, such as turfgrass seeds, moisture is necessary to increase P_{fr} concentrations. Thus, successful turf establishment, as related to P_{fr}, requires light and adequate moisture.

LOW LIGHT CONDITIONS

Shade causes significant growth changes in turfgrass plants. In response to shade, turfgrass plants form more of an upright growth habit including thinner, longer leaves; shallower rooting; lower plant energy levels; reduced tillering; and less dense stands. In turf, shade is commonly associated with trees but shading occurs between individual turfgrass plants as well. This competition between turfgrass plants is further described in this book in chapters addressing intra- and inter-specific turfgrass competition. The remaining part of this chapter examines shading effects caused by trees.

Shade is a major problem in areas where turfgrasses are grown beneath or in close proximity to trees, and its effects result in reduced amounts and quality of light received by the turf. Light transmitted through tree canopies comes through at longer wavelengths (far-red, infrared) which are not desirable for photosynthesis. (Figure 8) Photosynthetic rates are slower under shade and result in plants having lower carbohydrate reserves and shallower root systems. Research has also shown that shading reduces the amount of chlorophyll in lower parts of the canopy. (Biran and Bushkin-Harav, 1981)

The change in quality of light influences turfgrass growth by affecting phytochrome. (Figure 9) In unshaded, daylight areas, red wavelengths predominate and convert the phytochrome to its active state, P_{fr}. But in shaded, nighttime situations, far-red wavelengths predominate switching the phytochrome to an inactive state (P_r). The inactive state results in a lack of leaf expansion, increased stem elongation and reduced tillering.

Shading and tree type influences the quantity of light that the turf receives. Trees that cast a deep shade, such as maple and oak, reduce the quantity of light to a greater extent than open canopy trees such as ash, birch and locust. Deciduous trees filter the quality of light by inter-

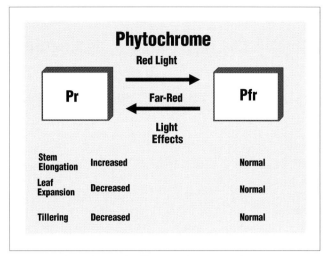

Figure 9. Phytochrome's effect on plant growth.

cepting the blues and reds and transmitting the far-reds. The exclusion of bluelight as the level of shade increases is the most critical wavelength missing for turfgrass growth. (McBee, 1969)

Turfgrass plants generally adapted to shade have a **low light compensation point** which is the light level at which net photosynthesis equals zero. In other words, the point where photosynthesis equals respiration. Plant growth, as measured by dry weight, occurs only when the light is above the compensation point. The ability of shade grasses to maximize photosynthesis at lower light intensities and lower compensation points allows them to compete in shade situations. Conversely, turfgrasses that have higher light compensation points do not perform well due to insufficient light necessary to carry on photosynthesis.

Warm-season grasses (C4) are the least shade tolerant because of a higher light compensation point. Of the warm-season turfgrasses, centipedegrass has shown the best shade tolerance while St. Augustinegrass (cv. "Floratam") the least. (Barrios et al, 1986) In moderately shaded conditions, Kentucky bluegrass can show some decline because of powdery mildew. (See Table 2)

Management practices for shade grown turfgrasses should address changes in germination effects. Mowing heights should be raised to account for the longer, thinner leaves and reduced canopy density. In addition, care should be taken to minimize any scalping to low shade-tolerant turfgrasses. Shade sensitive turfgrasses have reduced levels of chlorophyll near the soil which decreases their recuperative capabilities and limits their ability to regenerate new tissue. Irrigate only when needed to promote deeper root systems and minimize overwatering. In shaded situations, promote air circulation to reduce humidity levels which will help reduce conditions favorable for disease development.

Light is critical for the development and growth of turfgrasses. Starting with the seed and progressing through to plant maturity, light is needed for energy, initiation of reproduction and seed germination. From a competitive standpoint, reduction in the quantity and quality of light limits, in general, turfgrass growth.

Ranking Turfgrass Species According to Shade Tolerance

Ranking	Cool-Season Turfgrasses	Warm-Season Turfgrasses
High	Fine Fescue Rough Bluegrass Annual Bluegrass	
Medium	Tall Fescue Perennial Ryegrass Kentucky Bluegrass Creeping Bentgrass	Centipedegrass St. Augustinegrass Zoysiagrass
Low		Bermudagrass

TABLE 1.

Powdery Mildew Resistant Cultivars

Species	Cultivars
Kentucky Bluegrass	A-34, Able I, America, Aquilla, Bristol, Eclipse, Enmundi, Glade, Harmony, Ram I, Mystic, Nugget, Welcome, Sydsport
Creeping Red Fescue	Boreal, Estica, Commodore, Dawson, Flyer, Fortress, Pernille, Robot, Ruby
Hard Fescue	Aurora, Biljart, Reliant, Scaldis, Spartan, Waldina
Chewings Fescue	Shadow
Sheep Fescue	Bighorn

TABLE 2.

(Source: J.M. DiPaolo, 1990)

3

Nutrients: Gases and Minerals As Resources

Facts are the air of science. Without them you never can fly. — Ivan Pavlov, Russian physiologist

OF THE SIXTEEN ELEMENTS essential for plant growth, carbon, oxygen and hydrogen are found in the largest amounts. (Figure 1, Table 1) Carbon, oxygen and hydrogen comprise 90 percent to 96 percent of a plant's dry weight. Turfgrass managers have little control over these three elements, yet their importance cannot be overlooked in turfgrass management.

Carbon, oxygen and hydrogen are involved in the construction of organic molecules (proteins, carbohydrates, etc.). Carbon comes from carbon dioxide in the air while oxygen comes from the air and water. Hydrogen is derived from the splitting of water during photosynthesis. (See Chapter 2) The remaining 13 elements are broken down into macro- and micronutrients. Macronutrients are found in the largest quantities of the plant while micronutrients are found in smaller quantities. These nutrients are discussed in greater detail under the section entitled nutrients.

GASES

Oxygen is critical for all living organisms since it plays a major role in aerobic respiration. Current oxygen levels, which comprise one-fifth of the atmosphere's volume, evolved as a byproduct of photosynthesis. Oxygen is normally not considered a limiting resource because it appears to be ubiquitous. (Figure 2) Due to the low solubility of oxygen in water, however, it may become limiting to turfgrass and organism growth. For example, if temperatures and microbial activity are high in golf course ponds and lakes, an excessive demand for oxygen known as biological oxygen demand (BOD) may occur. This causes a depletion of oxygen and results in death to aerobic organisms i.e., fish.

Additionally, a depletion of oxygen can occur in waterlogged soils. In soils where water levels are high and oxygen levels are low, root respiration is severely restricted to a point where water cannot be taken up. The end result is plant wilt. The likelihood of wet wilt occurring, a condition where plants wilt in the absence of oxygen, is

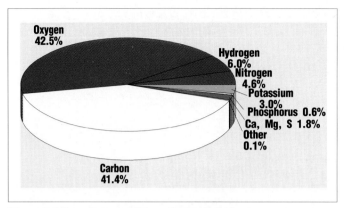

Figure 1. Mineral composition of a typical plant.

greatest in compacted soils. Compacted soils are characterized by an increase in solids (i.e., bulk density) and decrease in air space while the water content remains fairly stable. (Figure 3) The composition of soil air differs slightly from atmospheric air. In soil air, carbon dioxide and water vapor register higher than the slightly lower oxygen levels found in atmospheric air. A means of measuring reduced oxygen content in the soil is through oxygen diffusion rates (ODR). O'Neil and Carrow (1983) reported ODR levels well below acceptable rates for at least 53 hours after irrigation on a compacted soil, while ODR levels on a non-compacted soil returned to normal after five hours.

A reduction in oxygen levels in the soil influences nutrient uptake. Consequently, an oxygen loss in the soil results in reduced potassium, nitrogen and phosphorus uptake. Calcium and magnesium uptake are affected, but to a lesser extent. One positive aspect is that turfgrass plants appear to be more tolerant to reduced air and increased moisture in the soil than most agronomic crops. (Waddington 1969; see Chapter 4)

OZONE

Ozone (O_3) forms from the combination of ultraviolet light and oxygen. Ozone has received considerable attention over the last 25 years as both a pollutant and an

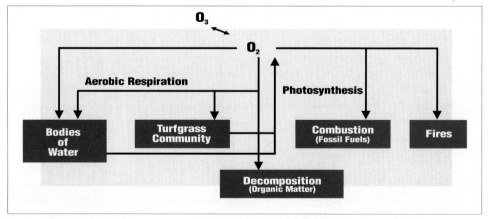

Figure 2. The oxygen cycle.

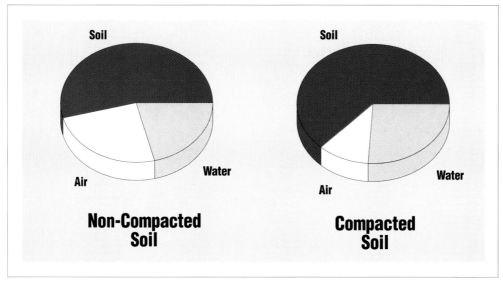

Figure 3. Comparison between non-compacted and compacted soils. Notice the decrease in air space in the compacted soil.

indispensable resource for life. Ozone forms a barrier — roughly 10 to 30 miles above the Earth's surface — that absorbs 99 percent of the ultraviolet light which can affect turfgrasses by causing alterations or mutations in their DNA. Ozone is a widespread pollutant in urban situations caused by incomplete combustion of industrial and automotive processes. Ozone affects plants by inhibiting growth, increasing respiration and decreasing photosynthesis. Leaf symptoms appear as a yellowish to tan necrosis while root growth is impaired. (Bennett and Runeckles, 1977) Warm-season turfgrasses are most resistant to ozone damage while cool-season turfgrasses such as Kentucky bluegrass, tall fescue and perennial ryegrass are intermediate. Annual bluegrass and creeping bentgrass are the most sensitive. (Richards et al, 1980; Brennan and Halisky, 1970) Cultivar sensitivity exists within species. Common types of Kentucky bluegrass are more sensitive to ozone than some improved cultivars (Richards et al, 1980) while genetic differences also exist in tall fescue. (Johnston et al, 1983)

Recently, the discovery of ozone depletion in the atmosphere through the introduction of chlorofluorocarbons (compounds that are used to propel droplets from spray cans; as a coolant for refrigerators and air conditioners;

Prolonged soil compaction and water saturation may cause a soil oxygen depletion and cause wet wilt. (Courtesy of William Daniel)

37

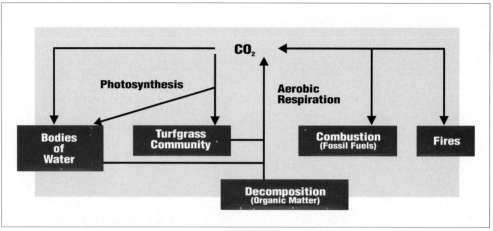

Figure 4. The carbon cycle.

and to create styrofoam) has caused worldwide concern. Chlorofluorocarbons, more specifically the chlorine from the compound, serve as an oxidant to react with the O_3 causing a breakdown. The depletion of the ozone layer will have global effects on human health and, on a smaller scale, turfgrass health.

CARBON DIOXIDE

Carbon dioxide provides the carbon source for organic molecules through photosynthesis. Aerobic respiration then results in carbon dioxide being released. (Equation 1)

Equation 1:

$$C_{12}H_{24}O_{12} + 12O_2 \longrightarrow 12CO_2 + 12H_2O$$

Carbon dioxide levels fluctuate during the day and seasons. When photosynthesis levels are high during daylight hours, carbon dioxide levels drop. At night, carbon dioxide absorption is low causing levels to increase. Over a seasonal period, carbon dioxide levels are low during actively growing periods and high during non-active periods such as winter.

Carbon dioxide is taken up by the plant through stomates. A conflict arises during periods of hot, dry weather since stomatal openings are a means of water escape during transpiration. If moisture is limited, stomates may close to conserve plant water and reduce carbon dioxide uptake. Thus, adequate moisture needs to be present for turfgrass plants to photosynthesize efficiently.

On a global scale, carbon dioxide has been a major culprit in the greenhouse effect. The greenhouse effect is a term used by scientists to describe the warming of the planet by the buildup of gases such as carbon dioxide, chlorofluorocarbons, methane and nitrous oxide. These gases allow light to reach the planet, but restrict the flow of infrared wavelengths back into space. As a result, these gases act like a blanket keeping the heat close to the earth. The buildup of these gases, especially carbon dioxide, are produced from fossil-burning activities and deforestation. (Figure 4)

The cycling of carbon from fixation via photosynthesis to its release as CO_2 is a fairly rapid process in turf, usually occurring within a year. Grass clippings are rapidly decomposed since they are mostly made up of water soluble compounds such as amino acids and proteins. (Bell, 1974) Initiated mainly for aesthetic purposes, turfgrass managers developed the habit of bagging clippings after mowing. Bagging clipings, however, has contributed to the landfill crisis in this country. Given the landfill crisis, banning the disposal of grass

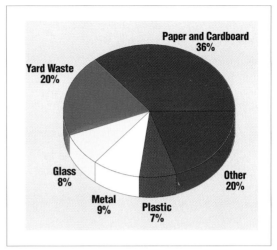

Figure 5. Major solid waste components of a landfill. (Source: Council for Solid Waste Solution)

clippings is a valid policy. (Figure 5) However, it is interesting to speculate what effects clippings disposal and the slow degrading process that occurs in these landfills would have on the carbon cycle. Do landfills act as a carbon sink, thus removing carbon that would normally escape into the atmosphere as CO_2?

Thatch may be of some benefit in capturing carbon for a longer period of time since it is composed of plant parts large in cellulose, hemicellulose and lignin. (Ledeboer and Skogley, 1967) These compounds are more difficult for microorganisms to degrade and consequently can serve as a longer term trap of carbon.

Researchers continue to study the effects of CO_2 on the warming of the planet. We

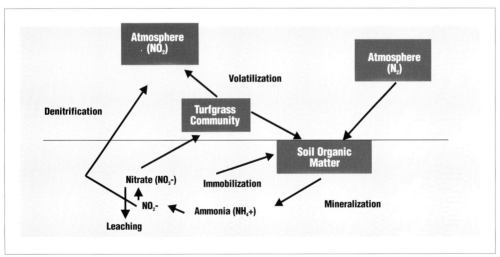

Figure 6. The nitrogen cycle.

know that carbon dioxide levels have been increasing for the past 30 years. What effect this may have on temperature is dependent on a number of factors: If the Earth is warming, the temperature of the oceans should be increasing. As ocean temperatures increase, however, the solubility of CO_2 increases resulting in the oceans dissolving greater amounts of CO_2. These interactions are complex and continued research is needed.

The effect of nitrogen on turfgrass growth, as shown here, in an improper application. Nitrogen promotes turfgrass growth and development, and enhances the color of the turf.

For turf science purposes, increasing CO_2 will have a major impact on the use of turfgrass species. Generally speaking, increasing CO_2 levels at moderate temperatures will increase growth of C3 plants to a greater extent than C4 plants. (Sionit et al, 1982) Associated with the increased CO_2 levels, however, is a rise in temperature which enhances the growth of C4 plants. If the greenhouse effect is viable, continued breeding research is needed to provide more drought- and salt-tolerant turfgrasses. A likely alternative is to breed for increased cold tolerance in warm-season turfgrasses, such as bermudagrass, to extend their range of adaptability.

NUTRIENTS

Nutritional balance in the plant is critical for survival and growth. How a turfgrass manager fertilizes can determine the susceptibility of plants to diseases, sensitivity to environmental stress, recuperative potential and wear tolerance. Nutrition is a consumable resource that requires replenishment to maintain and provide a healthy turf. Proper fertilization of turfgrasses is often a difficult practice to effectively accomplish. In row crops, fertilization programs are evaluated on yield while in turf, aesthetics and plant health are more difficult to quantify. However, an understanding of the role of the nutrients, timing and rate of application as well as the type of carrier can help make the decisions easier.

NITROGEN CYCLE

The nitrogen cycle is a dynamic process in which turfgrass managers can exert considerable influence. (Figure 6) A key step in the nitrogen cycle is mineralization. Nitrogen is tied up in organic forms that are unavailable for plant uptake. Microbes break down organic matter by splitting the organic molecules (large, proteins) into amino acids which are then used by the microorganism as low molecular weight nitrogen compounds.

Mineralization is a slow process that depends on carbon:nitrogen (C:N) ratios, temperature, moisture and pH. A high C:N ratio makes it difficult for microorganisms to break the molecule down without an additional nitrogen source. A desirable

C:N ratio for microbial decomposition ranges from 10:1 to 20:1. Temperature and moisture need to be optimum for microbial activity. Temperatures in the range of 75 to 95 F and adequate moisture are needed. Summer months have the greatest level of mineralization which, to the turfgrass manager, is beneficial. Even under low nitrogen fertility programs during the summer months, some nitrogen is made available from organic matter. Under warm temperatures, moisture is a limiting limiting factor in mineralization while in the fall and winter, temperature is limiting. Soil pHs below 4.5 reduce mineralization because microbial activity is inhibited.

The same principles of mineralization apply to nitrogen fertilizers. The quickly available sources provide readily available nitrogen while slow-release forms such as ureaformaldehyde (long-chain compounds) require microbial breakdown. In natural situations, the rate of mineralization is the limiting factor for plant growth. In managed turfgrass stands, the application of fertilizers eliminates mineralization as a limiting factor.

Once nitrogen is in a plant available form, four major fates within the nitrogen cycle become important. The first is uptake by the plant. In cool-season turfgrasses, recent research has shown that a quickly available nitrogen source is virtually depleted from the system within 48 hours after application. (Bowman et al, 1989) Bowman and his colleagues attributed this depletion to plant uptake.

Volatilization, especially with quick-release nitrogen sources, is a second means of nitrogen loss to the environment. (Titko et al, 1987) Volatilization is greatest when a leaf blade is moist, such as when urea is left on a leaf blade, followed by rapid drying. (Wesely et al, 1987) Volatilization can be reduced if irrigation is applied immediately after application. (Bowman et al, 1987; Titko et al,1987) Important in nitrogen volatilization from turf is the activity of the urease enzyme. Urease is found in the soil and thatch and catalyzes the reaction of urea to ammonia (NH_3). The greater the amount of urease present, the greater the likelihood of volatilization. The amount of urease is greater in thatch than in the underlying soil which could result in greater volatilization from thatchy turf. (Bowman et al,1987; Torello and Wehner, 1983)

These turf tests show a comparison among germinating perennial ryegrass (PR), annual bluegrass (AB) and creeping bentgrass (CB) varieties. The bottom photo has received a phosphorus application while the top photo has not.

41

Urease inhibitors phenylphosporodi-amidate (PPD); thiophophoric acid tra-imide (MBPT); and ammonium thiosul-fate (ATS) have been used on turf with limited success. However, recent work has shown the potential value of these types of compounds for increasing nitrogen efficiency and reducing volatilization with urea. (Joo et al, 1987; 1991)

Generally speaking, NBPT and PPD are substantially more effective in reducing nitrogen volatilization than ATS. It has been proposed that the cations magnesium and potassium, mixed with urea, might have the capabilities to reduce urease activity. Through turfgrass research, however, it has been determined that the use of potassium and magnesium for reducing volatilization has not been effective. (Joo et al, 1991)

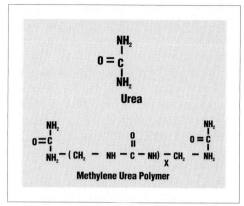

Figure 7. The chemical structure of urea and a methylene urea polymer. The length of the (CH_2 - NH - C NH)$_x$ component dictates the speed at which nitrogen releases (the longer the chain the slower the release).

Denitrification is the third means of nitrogen loss. Denitrification does not appear to be a serious problem in turf unless temperatures are high and the soil is water saturated. (Mancino et al, 1988) Turf under these conditions will appear chlorotic, and most likely in need of a nitrogen application.

The fourth possible fate is nitrate leaching. Nitrate leaching in turfgrass situations is minimal under soils containing silt and clay fractions. Geron et al (1992) found that minimal nitrogen leaching occurred on established turf under recommended fertility programs. Under newly constructed sites where soil had been disturbed, however, nitrate levels were high. This results from increased mineralization rather than from any effects caused by a turf treatment. However, mineralization quickly dropped off within a few months after each disturbance. On sandy soils, such as a putting green, careful nitrogen applications need to be made since significant nitrogen leaching has been reported. (Brown et al, 1982)

PHOSPHORUS

Phosphorus is a major component of adenosine triphosphate (ATP), an energy-rich compound used in numerous metabolic processes. The most critical time a plant needs phosphorous is during seedling establishment. Seeds require a large amount of energy to initially germinate and grow. At this point, applications of phosphorus will enhance seedling growth.

POTASSIUM

Potassium acts as a catalyse for a number of plant reactions. Its importance in turf is not fully understood, but it does appear to increase the wear tolerance of turfgrasses. Potassium is readily lost from the turfgrass system through leaching,

particularly in sandy soils. Potassium applications need to be made in a regular fashion in areas where potassium loss is a concern.

FERTILIZERS
A number of fertilizers are available for use on turf with nitrogen fertilizers being among the most numerous. From a turfgrass standpoint, the nitrogen source may influence the outcome of two competing species. In addition, the nitrogen source may influence the severity of turfgrass diseases. (Dernoeden, 1991) In Chapters 7 and 9, the influence of a nitrogen source on both turfgrass species and predator competition is explained. In this section, the major groups of nitrogen fertilizers are discussed. (Table 3)

Nitrogen fertilizers are classified as either quick- or slow-release products. Quick-release sources provide NO_3^- and NH_4^+ directly to the turf. The advantages to quickly available nitrogen are rapid initial plant response, ease of application, availability independent of environment and low cost. For the most part, quickly available sources are water soluble allowing for both liquid (with no agitation) and dry application. Once applied to the turf the nitrogen, in the form of nitrate or ammonium, is immediately available for uptake without having to undergo biotic activity to break the product down or wait for proper environmental conditions (i.e., moisture and/or temperature). The response from quick-release sources occurs within days after an application reflecting in increased growth and greener color.

The disadvantages to quick-release sources are high foliar burn potential; short residual; and increased leaching, volatility and runoff potential. Quick-release sources of nitrogen have a relatively high salt index. Salt index reflects the number of cations (NH_4^+) and anions (NO_3^-) on the foliage or in a solution. Due to osmotic potentials (i.e., water flows from low ion concentrations to high consistencies), these ions tend to draw water out of the plant resulting in burn. Generally, low-moisture conditions and high temperatures enhance burn potential. Quick-release sources provide nitrogen immediately to the turfgrass plant and can result in a flush of growth. This flush of growth lasts a relatively short period of time with the effects of the nitrogen wearing off within four weeks.

Slow-release sources discharge nitrogen over an extended period of time. The major advantages to slow-release products are low burn potential; lower risk of loss i.e., volatilization or leaching; less frequent applications; and a more uniform response. Disadvantages include slow initial plant response, higher cost and the need to apply product as a granular due to a lack of solubility.

Slow-release nitrogen products can be classified into three groups depending on their mechanism of release. The first group of products depends primarily on microbial decomposition. The majority of the products listed under this release mechanism are termed ureaformaldehyde (UF) fertilizers. These products are formed by reacting urea with formaldehyde. This reaction gives rise to methylene ureas that vary in their length (i.e., a combination of urea attached to a methylene group). (Figure 7) The longer the chain the slower the release of the product. In some instances, long-chain UF fertilizers may take years to release.

In the process of forming a UF fertilizer, a mix of short- and long-chain methylene ureas are combined with free urea to make up the product. Classification of the release of UF-type fertilizers is based on water solubility. Two temperatures, 22 C (cold water) and 100 C (hot water) are used.

Fraction 1. Cold-water soluble nitrogen (CWSN)—High solubility in water is the characteristic of this fraction group. The nitrogen consists of free urea and short-chain methylene ureas (methylene diurea and dimethylene triurea). Release characteristics of this fraction is rapid and similar to quick-release sources.

Fraction 2. Cold-water insoluble nitrogen (CWIN)—The nitrogen fraction within this group consists of slowly available nitrogen and intermediate length methylene ureas (trimethylene tetraurea and tetramethylene pentaurea). Nitrogen release is over a period of several weeks.

Fraction 3. Hot water insoluble nitrogen (HWIN) — The nitrogen fraction contained in this group releases so slowly (over a period of years) that a large percentage are undesirable. Long-chain methylene ureas (pentamethylene hexaurea and longer chains) characterize this group.

A common term used to describe the slow-release characteristics of a fertilizer is WIN which stands for Water Insoluble Nitrogen. The WIN value indicates the percentage of Fractions 2 and 3 in the fertilizer. However, it does not tell the percentage of each fraction. The activity index (AI) provides the relative amount of CWIN and HWIN. The AI value is calculated using the following formula:

$$AI = \frac{\% \ CWIN - \% \ HWIN}{\% \ CWIN}$$

The higher the AI value the less amount of HWIN is present. An effective UF-type fertilizer should have an AI value greater than 40. A value less than 40 results in too much HWIN making the release too slow.

Additional slow-release sources dependent on microbial degradation are the natural organics. These products are predominantly byproducts of plant, animal and waste processes. The nitrogen is contained in complex organic compounds that are not particularly soluble in water. Nitrogen release is dependent on microbial breakdown. Amending natural organic fertilizers with an innoculum of soil microrganisms and enzymes that may hasten nitrogen release have, so far, been ineffective. (Peacock and Daniel, 1992; Peadcock and DiPaola, 1992)

The second group of slow-release products depend on water solubility for nitrogen release. The slow dissolution of the particle gives these types of fertilizers slow-release characteristics. In turf, isobutyledene diurea (IBDU) is currently the only product classified in this group. The release rate of this product is dependent on particle size and soil moisture. The smaller the particle the faster it will dissolve. Soil moisture is critical because the more water present the faster the release.

The IBDU slow-release nitrogen fraction is described as WIN. As previously mentioned with UF-type fertilizers, the WIN fraction is made up of long- and short-chain methylene ureas. However, with IBDU the WIN fraction is of uniform composition. The particles are screened into two sizes: 0.5-1.00 mm (fine) and 0.7-2.5 mm (coarse).

The last group of slow-release fertilizers are products that encapsulate a urea particle. The breakdown of the coat over time releases the nitrogen. Currently there are two products available. The first is sulfur-coated urea (SCU) — free urea which is heated and sprayed with molten sulfur that coats the particle. The particle is then coated with a sealant. Release is dependent on defects in the coating. The slow-release effect comes from the staggered breakdown of the product. Once the coating is broken, free urea is present. Temperature, soil moisture and microbial activity influence SCU release.

Release characterization is determined by the seven-day dissolution rate. A known weight (50 grams) is placed in 250 ml of water at 38 C. Urea in solution at seven days is measured and expressed as a percentage of the total urea content. A seven-day dissolution rate of 20 percent to 30 percent is desirable for an initial response. The seven-day dissolution rate has correlated well with field studies when each SCU product is evaluated separately. (Hummmel and Waddington, 1986) Some care should be practiced with this product. Once the coating is broken, free urea is present. Any practice that may mechanically break the particle prematurely should be avoided.

The second type of encapsulated fertilizer is the resin-coated urea — urea encapsulated with a resin cover. This fertilizer can be formulated to give short- to long-day release characteristics. The most uniform response with resin-coated ureas has been reported as a 100-day release with a 270-day release product being considered too slow. (Hummel, 1989)

In summary, nutrition is important in the development and growth of turfgrass plants. It is a limiting resource dependent on proper application by the turfgrass manager. In the coming chapters, nutrition will be important in the competitive outcome of turfgrass species. In regard to nitrogen, the fertilizer, the form (nitrate or ammonia) and the amount present will affect the outcomes of turfgrass species, and influence pest severity on the turf.

The Essential Mineral Plant Nutrients

Macro	Micro
Nitrogen (N)	Zinc (Zn)
Potassium (K)	Copper (Cu)
Phosphorus (P)	Molybdenum (Mo)
	Chlorine (Cl)
Sulfur (S)	Boron (B)
Magnesium (Mg)	Iron (Fe)
Calcium (Ca)	Manganese (Mn)

TABLE 1.

Essential Elements Necessary for Turfgrass Growth

Element	Uptake Form	Transportability	Plant Function
N	NO_3^-, NH_4^+	good, throughout plant	Component of amino acids, proteins, chlorophyll, nucleic acids and co-enzymes. Affects root growth, color, density, disease proneness and recuperative potential.
P	HPO_4^{-2}, HPO_4^-	good, throughout plant	Component of nucleic acids, ADP, ATP and phospholipids. Important nutrient for establishment and root growth.
K	K^+	good, throughout plant	Activates enzymes used in protein, sugar, starch synthesis and as most ions do, maintains turgor pressure. Potassium is associated with improving wear and stress tolerance.
S	SO_4^{-2}	good in organic form, poor as an ion	Component of some amino acids, vitamins, most proteins. Sulfur deficiencies result in impaired growth.
Ca	Ca^{+2}	poor, fixed to cell walls	Important as a cementing agent to keep cell walls together. Necessary component for spindle formation in meiosis and mitosis.
Mg	Mg^{+2}	good	Component of chlorophyll, activates a number of enzymes used in photosynthesis, respiration, protein synthesis.
Fe	Fe^{+2}, Fe^{+3} chelated	poor, inactivated in plant by an excess of Mn	Involved in the synthesis of chlorophyll; component of electron transport systems.
Mn	Mn^{+2}, Mn^- chelated	poor, excessive use of iron can cause deficiency in tissue	Acts as co-enzyme for many enzymes.
Cu	Cu^{+2}, Cu^- chelate	poor, high concentrations toxic	Component of enzymes used in carbohydrate and protein metabolism.

Zn	Zn^{+2}, Zn^- chelated	poor, high concentrations toxic	Used in formation of auxins, chloroplasts and starch. Component of some enzymes.
Mo	MoO_4^{-2}	poor, accumulate in leaf tissue	Essential in enzyme reaction that reduces nitrate, and component of enzyme used for nitrogen fixation.
Cl	Cl^-	good	Aids in photosynthesis, minor role in plants.
B	HBO_3^{-2}, H_2BO_3	poor, concentrates in leaf tips	Affects cell division, nitrogen metabolism, water relations, hormone movement.

TABLE 2.   *(Adapted from Larcher, W. 1975. Physiological Plant Ecology.)*

47

Some Common Nitrogen Sources Used on Turfgrasses

Form	Trade Name	Fertilizer Grade	Total N	WIN
Soluble Solids	Monoammonium phosphate	10-50-0	10	0
	Diammonium phosphate	18-46-0	18	0
	Ammonium nitrate	33.5-0-0	33.5	0
	Calcium nitrate	20-0-0	20	0
	Sodium nitrate	16-0-0	16	0
	Potassium nitrate	13-0-44	13	0
	Urea	46-0-0	46	0
Slow-release solids	Milorganite	6-2-0	6	5.5
	Nitroform Blue Chip	38-0-0	38	27.0
	IBDU (coarse)	31-0-0	31	27.9
	IBDU (fine)	31-0-0	31	26.3
	Methylene ureas	---	38-41	10-14
	Sulfur-coated urea	---	32-38	---
	Resin-coated fertilizer	variable		
	Melamine	variable		
	Organic Sources	variable		
Solutions	RESI-GROW 4340	30-0-0	30	0
	RESI-GROW 4341	30-0-2	30	0
	Formulene LU	30-0-1	30	0
	N-SURE	28-0-0	28	0
	Nitro-26	26-0-0	26	0
	NBN	30-0-0	30	0
Suspension	Homogesol-27	27-0-0	27	2.7
	Slow-Release	18-0-1	18	4.5
	FLUF	18-0-0	18	4.5
	RESI-GROW 4318	18-0-0	18	4.5
	U-WIN	18-0-0	18	4.5
	Nutralene	40-0-0	40	14.5
Sprayable Powders	Methylene Urea	41-0-0	41	12
	Nitroform Powder Blue	38-0-0	38	25
	IBDU	31-0-0	31	23

TABLE 3.   *(Source: J.R. Street)*

Water: As A Resource

Water is the principle, or the element, of things.
— Aristotle, philosopher

TURFGRASS GROWTH and survival is dependent on the presence of moisture. Plants contain from 75 percent to nearly 90 percent water by weight, but a decrease in water content by only 10 percent can cause turfgrass death.

Of the water absorbed, only 1 percent to 3 percent is used in metabolic processes. The remaining water is lost through transpiration. It is estimated that 600 pounds of water is required to produce 1 pound of dry matter. To plants, water is: a vital constituent of the protoplasm; required for photosynthetic activities; the end product of respiration; the transport medium for nutrients, organic compounds and gases; and a moderator of temperature change of the protoplasm. (Beard, 1973) Turfgrasses receive water from precipitation (such as rain and snow), water vapor, dew and irrigation.

TRANSPIRATION

The vast majority of water used by plants is for transpiration. Transpiration is a cooling process in which water evaporates from the leaf (liquid) to the atmosphere (gas). Just as the evaporation of perspiration cools people, the evaporation of water from the leaf surface cools the plant. The driving force for transpiration is the vapor pressure gradient that exists between the atmosphere and the leaf. Vapor pressure, caused by the presence of water vapor in the air, is one part of total air pressure. Air at high relative humidity has more water vapor (higher vapor pressure) than air at low relative humidity. A leaf of a well-watered plant is considered to have a relative humidity of about 100 percent. The air around the leaf often has a relative humidity of less than 100 percent. This establishes a vapor pressure gradient between the leaf and the air and causes water to evaporate from the leaf.

The difference between leaf vapor pressure and air vapor pressure results in the vapor pressure gradient. For example, if the relative humidity in the leaf is 100 percent at a leaf temperature of 77 F, the vapor pressure is 23.76 mm mercury (Hg). (Table 1) Vapor pressure may be expressed as the height of a column of Hg that particular amount of water vapor will support. If, at the same time, the air temperature is 77 C, but the relative humidity is 40 percent, the vapor pressure of the air is 9.50 mm Hg. The difference (23.76 - 9.50) is the vapor pressure deficit. The greater the vapor pressure deficit, the higher the transpiration rate.

In shaded situations the turfgrass temperature is lower while the relative humidity of the air is typically higher, compared to full sun situations outside the shaded area. The vapor pressure gradient in the shade is lower than in full sun. This is shown numerically as (hypothetical example):

	Full Sunshine (30C = 86F)	Partial Shade (25C = 77F)
Leaf Relative Humidity	100	100
Leaf Vapor Pressure (mm Hg)	31.82	23.76
Air Relative Humidity	40	40
Air Vapor Pressure (mm Hg)	9.5	9.5
Vapor Pressure Gradient	22.32	126

Consequently, the transpiration rate and water use will be lower in the shade than in the full sun.

Water is not lost uniformly from the leaf surface. Resistance to transpiration comes from the boundary layer, the cuticle and the stomata. The boundary layer is a thin area of air that develops along the leaf surface. The thicker the layer the greater the resistance to transpiration. Thickness of the boundary layer is influenced by wind velocity, relative humidity and leaf shape. Narrow small leafs have thinner boundary layers than larger thicker leaves. (see Chapter 5)

The cuticle is a waxy layer that coats the outer surface of the leaf. It greatly reduces water loss so that most of the waste occurs through the stomata. As previously mentioned, stomata are openings in the leaf that allow CO_2 to enter and water vapor to leave. Stomata comprise only 2 percent to 3 percent of the leaf surface. Yet, as much as 90 percent of the water vapor transpired passes through stomata. Each stoma is surrounded by two guard cells. Guard cells are capable of opening stomata when they are turgid and closing them when they dry. Stomatal openings are influenced by light intensity (open to light, closed to dark); moisture stress (closed); and temperature (under extreme temperatures will close). In addition, some chemicals such as antitranspirants reduce plant transpiration by closing stomata.

Water is necessary for plant survival.

WATER FORMATION ON TURF

Dew is the term used to describe the

formation of water on the leaf blade early in the morning. Two types of dew may occur: condensation and guttation. Condensation occurs when the leaves are cooler than the air. If the moist air around the leaf is cooled to its dew point, water vapor condenses on the leaves. If the temperature goes below freezing, frost forms.

Guttation occurs when water pressure builds up in the roots causing plant water to exude from openings called hydathodes. Guttation occurs most often in the spring when soil

Dew is a term used to describe moisture and guttation on the leaf blade.

moisture levels are high and transpiration rates are low. Guttation water is high in organic compounds (amino acids) and results in the leaf remaining wet for a longer period of time. Endo (1967) found that nutrients in guttation water increased the growth of fungi, and consequently increased the likelihood of disease. The removal of guttation by dragging the turf with a hose or lightly applying water speeds up the leaf drying process and removes a potential food source for pathogens from the leaf blade in turf.

WATER ABSORPTION
Under normal conditions limited water is absorbed through the leaves. Leaf absorption is of minor consequence unless the turf is wilting or under drought stress. The amount of water absorbed through leaves under these conditions may be a critical factor in turf survival. The vast majority of water absorption occurs in the root hair region of the roots. Root hairs are long projections of root cells that extend from the roots near the root tip, and are the primary mechanism of water and nutrient absorption. Root hairs live only a few weeks, but new root hairs form on elongating roots. Thus, an actively growing root system enhances water absorption.

The amount of water absorbed by the roots depends on the depth of the root system, the root number, the root extension rate, the amount of water available, the transpiration rate and the soil temperature. The deeper the root system and the greater the growth (root number and root extension rate), the greater the potential for water uptake. Transpiration affects how much water is used because most of the water absorbed by the roots is lost through transpiration. Soil temperature is important in that it influences root activity. The colder the temperature, the less root activity and the slower the water uptake. Warm-season grasses are more sensitive to cool soil temperatures than cool-season grasses.

WATER-USE RATE
Water-use rate is defined as the total amount of water required for turfgrass growth in addition to the quantity transpired from the grass plant and evaporated from the

soil surface. It is typically measured as evapotranspiration and expressed in millimeters per day. Water-use rate is important when designing irrigation requirements for turfgrasses, however, it's not a measure of drought resistance. For example, tall fescue is considered a good turfgrass for drought situations, yet its water-use rate is as high as creeping bentgrass, annual bluegrass and Kentucky bluegrass. (Table 2) Tall fescue is drought resistant because it is able to tap into water deeper in the soil profile due to its down-reaching root system.

Initial turfgrass wilt systems appear as a bluish color. The addition of water will alleviate wilt systems.

Turfgrasses that have generally low evapotranspiration rates are characterized as having high canopy resistance (high shoot density and horizontal leaf orientation) and a low leaf area (slow vertical leaf growth and narrow leaf blade) (Kim and Beard, 1988). Under non-limiting water conditions, the stomatal density of turfgrasses appears to have no correlation with evapotranspiration. (Green et al, 1990)

In some instances, evapotranspiration rates vary among cultivars of the same turfgrass species. Shearman (1986) has reported as much as a 64 percent difference in evapotranspiration rates among Kentucky bluegrass cultivars and similar results with perennial ryegrass cultivars (Shearman, 1989) and to a lesser degree with tall fescue (Kopec et al, 1988). Among tall fescues, turf-type tall fescue had lower evapotranspiration rates than the forage-type tall fescue. Variability does occur in the methodology in which evapotranspiration rates are measured. For example, evapotranspiration rates among zoysiagrass cultivars did not differ in a field study in Texas. (Green et al, 1991) Yet, under growth chamber conditions, differences among zoysiagrass cultivars occurred.

Weeds affect the overall evapotranspiration rate of a turfgrass stand. Smooth crabgrass and yellow foxtail exhibit evapotranspiration rates similar to Kentucky bluegrass. (Fry and Butler, 1989) Barnyardgrass has a lower evapotranspiration rate while white clover has a higher evapotranspiration rate than Kentucky bluegrass. From a management perspective, the eradication of weeds such as white clover may be an effective means of reducing evapotranspiration rates. (Frey and Butler, 1989)

WATER DEFICITS

If not watered adequately during the course of a growing season, turf may be exposed to water deficits. These deficits vary in severity and duration. How the grass plant responds to water deficits explains, to a great extent, the survivability of the turf.

Wilt is the drooping, rolling or folding of turfgrass leaves resulting from a loss of turgidity. It occurs when the transpiration rate is greater than the rate of water absorption by the roots, but it is only temporary and can be corrected with the application of water. Wilt symptoms appear as a bluish-green color. **Wet wilt** is the wilting of the turf when soil moisture is high. In situations where soils are waterlogged, roots cannot take up moisture because of a deficiency of oxygen. Wet wilt occurs most often on waterlogged, compacted soils in turfgrasses with restricted root systems such as annual bluegrass and rough bluegrass. During periods of wet wilt, light applications of water may provide foliar uptake and provide some relief. However, reducing compaction and improving drainage in sites where wet wilt occurs should be attempted.

Drought is a prolonged water stress that limits or prevents turfgrass growth. Drought severity depends on the duration of periods without rainfall/irrigation, the evaporation power of the air and the water holding capacity of the soil. The ability of turfgrass plants to withstand drought conditions is referred to as drought resistance. Drought resistance is defined as:

Drought Resistance = Drought Tolerance + Drought Avoidance

Drought tolerance is the ability of a turfgrass plant to sustain biochemical and physiological processes in the face of an internal decrease in water content. Turfgrass plants are very sensitive to protoplasmic desiccation and the tolerance range is narrow.

Drought avoidance is defined as the ability to sustain internal plant water levels through morphological and physical features of growth. Examples of drought avoidance mechanisms include more efficient and deeper root systems to gain access to soil moisture reserves; effective stomata closure and mechanisms to prevent transpiration

The lack of irrigation water has resulted in a drought situation on this golf course fairway.

through the cuticle; and a reduction in transpiration surface. Characteristics of leaves that develop under conditions of poor water availability include low specific leaf areas,* closer stomatal spacing, narrower leaves, closer vein spacing and thicker cuticle and epidermis.

$$* \text{ specific leaf area} = \frac{\text{surface area (dm2)}}{\text{fresh weight of leaf (g)}}$$

Additional means of avoiding drought include using turfgrass plants that go dormant in the absence of moisture, and by the completion of a plant's life cycle before drought occurs. Dormancy is the suspension of outwardly visible activity caused by environmental conditions. Rejuvenation of the plant comes with the regeneration of new leaves from the crown. Some turfgrasses such as annual bluegrass (the annual biotype) completes its life cycle before drought conditions occur. Annual bluegrass produces massive amounts of seedheads in the spring, but the plant dies once dry hot conditions occur. When favorable conditions return, seeds germinate.

Osmotic drought occurs when an internal water deficit is caused by a high external salt condition. High salt concentrations such as those found in saline/sodic soils make water uptake difficult even if moisture is present. A similar type of injury occurs with fertilizer burn. Salt from the fertilizer may draw water from the leaf or root if the salt is left in contact with the plant. The potential for a water-stressed turfgrass plant being more prone to fertilizer burn is not likely. (Johnson and Christians, 1985) Thus, fertilizers can be applied to a water-stressed turf and or dormant turf without increasing the likelihood of burn. A slower-release source may be advisable, however, to reduce the likelihood of fertilizer burn from a quick-release source.

EXCESSIVE WATER

Flooding can cause severe damage to turf by accelerating soil erosion; depositing soil, salt and debris on the turf; and causing direct submersion injury. The extent of submersion injury is dependent on the turfgrass species, duration, depth, environmental conditions and health of the plant. Submersion injury is not considered a major problem on turfgrasses unless the plants are exposed to high water temperatures. (Beard and Martin, 1970) In situations where water is shallow and stagnant, the temperature of the water will rise quickly causing potential turfgrass damage. In situations where the water is flowing over turf, temperatures will rise slowly creating less potential for turfgrass injury. In general, creeping bentgrass is more tolerant to flooding than Kentucky bluegrass and annual bluegrass, with fine fescue being the least tolerant. Of the warm-season turfgrasses, Bahiagrass and bermudagrass are most tolerant to submersion, while zoysiagrass and St. Augustinegrass are less tolerant. Centipedegrass is least tolerant. Improving drainage in areas that are prone to flooding will reduce the chance of turfgrass damage by minimizing depth and duration of submersion.

WINTER DAMAGE CAUSED BY MOISTURE

During the winter plant water uptake is curtailed by reduced root activity and/or frozen soil water. If turf is exposed to open, windy areas, a lack of moisture uptake may cause plant damage. Desiccation is the term used to reflect the dehydration of tissues. When turf desiccates, the leaves turn white due to a combination of dry atmospheric conditions and low soil moisture availability. Desiccation is of notable concern in late winter if the soil has not thawed, but the sun begins to warm the leaves resulting in transpiration. Winter desiccation may be prevented by providing adequate moisture in the fall, installing windbreaks, late-season topdressing or installing synthetic covers.

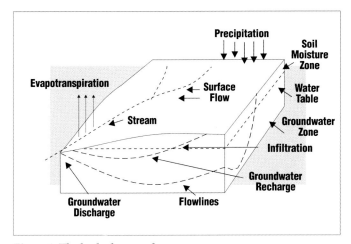

Figure 1. The hydrology cycle.

Traffic should be minimized on frozen or wet slushy turf in the winter. Heavy traffic on excessively wet turf can cause the slush to be forced into contact with the plant crown. If the crown hydrates, a quick drop in temperature can rupture the crown causing death. On frozen soils, traffic can cause pressure to frozen tissue causing a disruption of the protoplasm. As long as the crown is unaffected, this is generally considered only a foliar problem. With the onset of warm temperatures the plant should recover. Further discussion of winter damage to turf is found in Chapter 5.

WATER QUALITY

Water quality is a concern of turf managers from two perspectives. One concern is what affects do turf management practices such as pesticide and fertilizer applications have on groundwater? The second concern is the quality of irrigation water used to keep the turf green as a supplement to natural rainfall. With both of these concerns, water quality is judged by the contaminates contained in the water. (Tables 3 and 4)

To understand how turfgrass management practices affect water quality, an understanding of the hydrology cycle is needed. (Figure 1). Turfgrass plants receive water in the form of precipitation. Once the water hits the soil surface it can be taken up by the plant, enter the soil, flow over the soil or return to the atmosphere through evaporation. Water that moves across the surface via runoff may carry nutrients or pesticides bound on soil particles to streams or ponds.

The amount of runoff in traditional agricultural settings is dependent on soil texture and slope. If the soil is high in clay (low percolation rate), the likelihood of runoff is greater particularly on sloping areas. Watschke (1990) has investigated the effects of runoff in turf and found that on established turf, movement of soil particles in runoff is almost non-existent. He also found that the amount of actual runoff from a turfgrass stand is small.

The second source of water movement is downward through the soil profile via infiltration. Soils that have a high sand content accept water more readily than soils high in clay. Movement through the soil profile is termed unsaturated flow. Once water reaches the water table it moves into the groundwater supply and travels via saturated flow. Downward movement of water may result in potential leaching of fertilizers and pesticides.

Cohen (1990), who monitored groundwater wells on four golf courses in Cape Cod, Mass., found that seven common turfgrass pesticides were not present and no currently registered pesticides were detected at toxicologically significant concentrations. However, in a recent study by the Environmental Protection Agency, municipal contamination of groundwater was found to be greater than rural. (Anonymous, 1990) In addition, the metabolite of the common turfgrass herbicide DCPA has been found at significant levels. Turf management practices for established turf stands rarely contribute to water pollution. This is not to say that turf managers have no need for concern. Protecting the environment is a goal of all, and the misuse of pesticides and fertilizers can only result in some form of environmental contamination.

IRRIGATION WATER

A suitable water source for irrigation presents a special problem for turfgrass managers. In some regions, residential and large turf areas have unrestricted access to water. However, especially in the West, water sources are often restricted and the quality of water is low (non-potable sources). The primary sources for irrigation water are ponds, wells and in residential areas, effluent water. The suitability of the

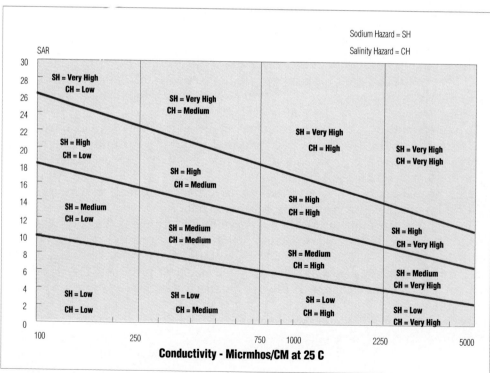

Figure 2. Classification of irrigation water. (Agricultural Handbook No. 60)

water source is dependent on measurable characteristics. (Table 4)

Water is of vital concern in most arid regions. Salt content is of special interest because high concentrations of salt can have a direct effect on turfgrass growth. The salinity of water is measured by electrical conductivity. If the conductivity is greater than 0.75 millimhos/cm, salinity is a problem. If conductivity is greater than 3.0 millimhos/cm, the water should not be used for irrigation. (Harivandi, 1988) The frequency and amount of irrigation water containing appreciable amounts of salt will also influence turfgrass survival. If an irrigation source high in salt is applied to a soil containing appreciable amount of salt, the ability of turfgrass plants to survive becomes more difficult. (Table 5)

Sodium adsorption ratio (SAR) directly measures the sodium content of the water. High sodium waters can cause dispersion of soil particles resulting in the destruction of soil characteristics. Using the United States Department of Agriculture (USDA) handbook number 60, the suitability of irrigation water can be determined. (Figure 2) For example, if a water quality test report comes back with the following information:

$$Ca^{++} = 40$$
$$Mg^{++} = 24$$
$$Na^{+} = 46$$

these values can be converted to milliequivalents per liter by dividing each cation by their milliequivalent weights (calcium = 20; magnesium = 12; and sodium = 23). The SAR value is then calculated using the equation in Table 4, which is:

$$SAR = 2 \: / \: [(2 + 2)/2]^{1/2}$$
$$SAR = 1.41$$

In this case, the SAR value of 1.41 would be low and pose no detrimental effect to the turfgrass plant. The electrical conductivity of the water indicates the salinity hazard. If, in the above example, the electrical conductivity of the water was 120 micromhos/cm, the water would not pose a risk for irrigation purposes. The USDA description of each classification is as follows:

Sodium Adsorption Ratio
1) low = water that can be used to irrigate almost any soil
2) medium = an appreciable sodium hazard exists for fine-textured soils with a high cation exchange capacity
3) high = water that may produce harmful levels of sodium; soil management practices such as applications of gypsum may be required
4) very high = water is unsuitable for irrigation, except maybe on low salinity soils
Electrical Conductivity

1) low = water has a low salinity hazard
2) medium = water can be used if moderate leaching occurs
3) high = water should not be used on soils of poor drainage; salt sensitive turfgrass species should not be used with this water
4) very high = water should not be used for irrigation

In summary, the amount and quality of water is critical for the survival of turfgrass species. In future chapters, competition for water as a limiting resource will be explored.

Vapor Pressure at Selected Temperatures and Relative Humidities

Temp F(C)	Vapor pressure (mm Hg) at indicated relative humidity									
	10%	20%	30%	40%	50%	60%	70%	80%	90%	100%
32 (0)	0.46	0.92	1.37	1.83	2.29	2.75	3.21	3.66	4.12	5.48
41 (5)	0.65	1.31	1.96	2.62	3.27	3.92	4.58	5.23	5.89	6.54
50 (10)	0.92	1.84	2.76	3.68	4.60	5.53	6.45	7.37	8.29	9.21
59 (15)	1.28	2.56	3.84	5.12	6.40	7.67	8.95	10.23	11.51	12.79
68 (20)	1.75	3.51	5.26	7.02	8.77	10.52	12.28	14.03	15.79	17.54
77 (25)	2.38	4.75	7.13	9.50	11.88	14.26	16.63	19.01	21.38	23.76
86 (30)	3.18	6.36	9.55	12.73	15.91	19.09	22.27	25.46	28.64	31.82
95 (35)	4.22	8.44	12.65	16.87	21.09	25.31	29.53	33.74	37.96	42.18

TABLE 1.   (*Source: Hammer, 1986*)

Ranking of Potential Evapotranspiration Rates for Major Turfgrasses

Relative Ranking	PET rate (mm/day)	Cool-Season	Warm-Season
Very low	<6		Buffalograss
Low	6-7		Bermudagrass Centipedegrass Zoysiagrass Blue grama
Medium	7-8.5	Hard Fescue Chewings Fescue Red Fescue	Bahiagrass Seashore Paspalum St. Augustinegrass Zoysiagrass (Emerald)
High	8.5-10		Perennial Ryegrass
Very High	>10	Tall Fescue Creeping Bentgrass Annual Bluegrass Kentucky Bluegrass Annual Ryegrass	

TABLE 2.

(Source: Beard, 1986)

Suggested Surface-Water Standards for Drinking Water

Characteristic	Permissible Standard
Physical:	
Color	75
Odor	not available
Turbidity	3
Microbial:	
Coliform organisms	10,000/100ml
Fecal coliforms	2,000/100ml
Inorganic chemicals (mg/l):	
Ammonia	0.5 (as N)
Arsenic	0.05
Barium	1.0
Boron	1.0
Cadmium	0.01
Chloride	250
Chromium	0.5
Copper	1.0
Dissolved oxygen	>= 4 (monthly mean)
Fluoride	0.8-1.7
Hardness	treated for
Iron	0.3
Lead	0.05
Manganese	0.05
Nitrates	10.0 (as N)
pH	6.0-8.5
Selenium	0.01
Silver	0.05
Sulfate	250
Total dissolved solids	500
Zinc	5.0
Organic Chemicals:	
Foaming agents	0.5
Oil and grease	virtually absent
Pesticides:	
Endrin	0.0002
Lindane	0.004
Methoxychlor	0.1
Toxaphene	0.005
Herbicides:	
2,4-D	0.1
2,4,5-TP	0.01

TABLE 3.

(Source: Hammer, 1986)

Characteristics for Deciding Suitability of Water Sources

Characteristic	Description
Total Dissolved Salts (TDS)	Expressed in mg/l. It is a measurement that is useful in defining a municipal or industrial wastewater. Classification of waters can be made using TDS: $\quad\quad\quad\quad$ TDS(mg/l) Fresh $\quad\quad\quad$ 0 - 1000 Brackish $\quad\quad$ 1000-10,000 Saline $\quad\quad\quad$ 10,000-100,000 Brine $\quad\quad\quad$ >100,000
pH	A measure of hydrogen ion concentration or acidity. Most natural waters will have pHs between 6 and 8. pH is of no direct benefit, but is a good indicator that problems exist if the water is too acid or basic.
Biological Oxygen Demand (BOD)	BOD by definition measures the quantity of oxygen utilized by a mixed population of microorganisms in the aerobic respiration. A high BOD may indicate the presence of sewage. BOD should be < 25 mg/l.
Hardness	A measure of the water's potential to form scale precipitates. Expressed as mg/l of $CaCO_3$.
Electrical Conductivity	A measure of the sample's ability to conduct electricity. Conductivity is directly proportional to salinity. It is measured as micromhos/cm or millimhos/cm.
Sodium Adsorption Ratio (SAR)	Expresses the predominance of sodium relative to calcium and magnesium. $SAR = Na^+ / [(Ca^{2+}+Mg^{2+})/2]^{1/2}$ Values needed to calculate SAR need to be expressed in milliequivalents (meq.) per liter. The conversion is meq/l = ppm/equivalent weight. Equivalent weights for Na, Ca and Mg are 23, 20 and 12.
Cation and Anion Concentrations	Expressed as mg/l or parts per million (ppm). Sum of cations should equal sum of anions.

TABLE 4.

Salt Tolerance Levels of Turfgrasses

Turfgrass	4 millmos/cm	4-8 millimos/cm	8-16 millimos/cm	16 millimos/cm
Cool-Season	Kentucky Bluegrass Colonial Bentgrass Creeping Red Fescue Annual Bluegrass Rough Bluegrass	Tall Fescue Perennial Ryegrass Chewings Fescue	Creeping Bentgrass	Alkaligrass
Warm-Season	Centipedegrass		Bermudagrass	Seashore Paspalum Zoysiagrass St. Augustine-grass

TABLE 5.

(Source: Harivandi, 1988)

5

Physiological Responses to Temperature

Science does not permit exceptions.
— Claude Bernard, French Scientist

AS THE DRIVING force for all biological functions temperature influences transpiration, water potential, the translocation of assimilates, metabolism, almost all enzymatic reactions, dormancy, growth and development. The ideal temperature range for turfgrass growth and development is narrow. For cool-season turfgrasses the optimum temperature range is 60 to 75 degrees F, and for warm-season turfgrasses the optimum range is 80 to 95 degrees F. Outside the optimum range, the health and competitive ability of turfgrasses can be detrimentally affected.

A leaf's temperature is dependent on the three elements defined in the following equation:

$$\text{Leaf Temperature} = \text{net radiation} - \text{convection} - \text{transpiration}$$

where **net radiation** is the difference between energy absorbed primarily from the sun but also from the surroundings, minus energy emitted either from reflection or transmission. Only 1 percent to 2 percent of the radiant energy hitting the leaf is used for photosynthesis. The remaining radiant energy must be disposed of to prevent temperature damage to the leaf. Absorption of radiant energy by the leaf increases temperature while energy emitted decreases leaf temperature. Fortunately, as the leaf temperature increases in response to radiant energy, the amount of energy emitted by the leaf increases sharply. The result is an increase in the leaf temperature, but at a slower rate than what is normally expected.

Convection is the transfer of heat from the leaf blade via air molecules. In this text, convection is used to encompass both convection and conduction. As the leaf temperature increases air molecules closest to the leaf blades absorb the energy and transmit it to adjacent air molecules (conduction). These excited air molecules increase in temperature, rise from the leaf blade and are replaced by less excited molecules or colder air (convection).

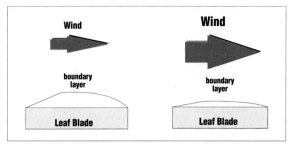

Figure 1. The affects of wind on the thickness of the boundary layer.

Resistance to convection comes from the boundary layer which is a thin layer of air next to the leaf surface. This layer restricts heat movement from the leaf. The thicker the boundary layer, the greater the resistance. Wind speed is a major factor in reducing the thickness of the boundary layer. (Figure 1)

Transpiration dissipates heat from the leaf through the cooling process of water evaporation. Resistance to transpiration is governed by the boundary layer and stomatal closings. Stomata significantly affect water loss through transpiration. During periods of plant water deficit, stomata close reducing transpiration and resulting in higher leaf temperatures.

PHYSIOLOGICAL RESPONSES

Photosynthesis and respiration are both sensitive to temperature. In the normal temperature range, incremental temperature escalations cause increased enzyme activity leading to greater photosynthetic activity. However, if temperatures continue to increase beyond an optimum temperature range enzyme activity diminishes causing a decrease in photosynthetic activity. (Figure 2) Respiration also continues to grow with increasing temperatures. When comparing photosynthesis and respiration responses at high temperatures, respiration will actually exceed photosynthesis. At some point, however, respiration decreases; usually above 104 F. High temperature stress can cause metabolic rate imbalance, respiratory depletion of substrates and reduce chloroplast photochemical activity. (Blum, 1988) At temperatures above 104 F, **denaturation** of enzymes begins to occur, and at 122 F proteins are inactivated.

Considerable research efforts have been undertaken to understand how plants respond internally to high temperature stress. One aspect of high temperature stress research has been the

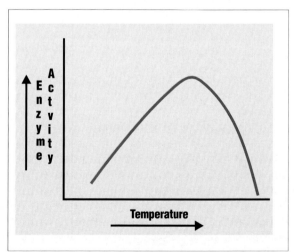

Figure 2. The relationship between enzyme activity and temperature. With increasing temperature, enzyme activity increases to a point. Beyond this point enzyme activity falls off rapidly.

study of a group of proteins called heat shock proteins. At temperatures above 104 F, plants produce heat shock proteins while at the same time, the vast majority of proteins normally produced under optimum temperature conditions is greatly curtailed. It is hypothesized that heat shock proteins are produced to protect the plant from high temperature by preventing proteins from denaturing. The production of heat shock proteins is dependent on a temperature acclimation phase. For example, if an immediate increase in temperature occurs, such as going from 82 F to 122 F, plant death will occur. However, if the plant is allowed to adapt (acclimate) to an intermediate temperature such as 104 F for a period of time before being subjected to 122 F, the plant survives. It is during the acclimation phase that heat shock proteins form. Fortunately, for turfgrass plants in the field gradual increases in temperature provide acclimation phases allowing for turfgrass survival at higher temperatures.

The improper application of a phenoxy herbicide to control clover on a creeping bentgrass green during a period of high temperature.

In some instances, however, a rapid increase in plant temperature may occur causing coagulation of the proteins. This results in a disruption of the protoplasm followed by rapid death to the turfgrass plant. High temperature stress leading to the death of the plant is often termed acute stress. Turfgrasses rarely encounter acute temperature stress in temperate regions unless they are established in extreme situations. For example, the placement of a synthetic cover on an athletic field is often done to keep rain off the field or to enhance seed germination. If the synthetic cover is left on the turf during periods of high light intensity and air temperatures, rapid turf death can occur. High temperature stress can also be seen on creeping bentgrass or annual bluegrass putting greens that received recent applications of heavy sand topdressings that had been left on the surface during a hot sunny day.

The likelihood of acute temperature stress is greater under conditions of restricted rates of transpiration due to droughty conditions. Under limited water situations and high temperatures, the leaf will close its stomates to reduce water loss. The elimination of transpiration as a leaf cooling mechanism may result in the leaf temperature increasing by 18 to 30 F.

Chronic high temperature stress is a more common form of stress related to high temperatures. Chronic stress occurs when an extended period of higher-than-normal temperatures exist. One particularly damaging aspect of chronic heat stress is the depletion of carbohydrate reserves. Carbohydrate depletion occurs when elevated temperatures cause more energy to be used in respiration than is being captured photosynthetically.

Chronic high temperatures affect root health by accelerating the root maturation process. As temperatures increase above the optimum roots elongate at a greater rate for a short period of time. This period of rapid root growth, however, is followed by rapid root mortality during prolonged periods of high temperatures. The problem is compounded by the partitioning of carbohydrates to shoots preferentially over roots which may result in less water uptake for the cooling process (transpiration).

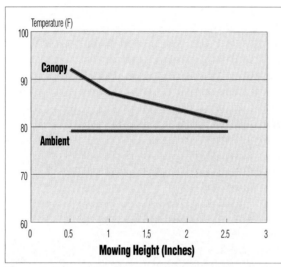

Figure 3. *Comparison between the canopy temperature of Kentucky bluegrass mowed at various heights and the ambient temperature. (Danneberger, unpublished data)*

Certain Kentucky bluegrass cultivars have genetic differences in how they allocate dry matter between roots and shoots which may provide an explanation for cultivar differences to heat stress. (Mehall et al, 1984; Goss and Law, 1967)

Chronic heat stress predisposes turfgrass plants to additional stresses. For example, the herbicide MCPP which is used on creeping bentgrass for clover control may cause severe damage during periods of high temperatures. Anthracnose, primarily a disease of annual bluegrass, occurs more readily when the turf is subjected to high temperature stress.

Detrimental effects of high temperature stress may be minimized through proper cultural practices. Turfgrass plants maintained under infrequent irrigation and low nitrogen levels are more heat tolerant than the same plants maintained under frequent irrigation and high nitrogen levels. From a competitive standpoint, differences in heat tolerance among turfgrass species is minimal if maintained at a high nitrogen level and irrigated frequently. For example, Kentucky bluegrass is considerably more heat tolerant than annual bluegrass when both are maintained with low nitrogen and infrequent irrigation. However, at high nitrogen levels and frequent irrigation, no difference in heat tolerance between the two species exists. (Wehner and Watschke, 1981)

Mowing practices can reduce or raise plant temperatures. For instance, raising the cutting height on turf during periods of high temperature leads to reduced canopy temperatures. (Figure 3) However, in high evapotranspiration situations such as those found in the western United States, Shearman (1989) warned that increasing the height of cut during high temperature periods may reduce the ability of the turf to survive. The additional foliar tissue generated by increasing the cutting height increases evapotranspiration requirements beyond that provided by a restricted root system under high temperature stress.

Scalping, which is the removal of an excessive amount of leaf tissue, should be avoided. If scalping occurs, the turf appears brown and stemmy and is slow to recover. Physiological repercussions to the plant are great. Carbohydrate reserves are needlessly drawn upon for shoot regrowth at the expense of long-term health during high temperature periods.

Syringing is the application of a light amount of water to a turf for the purpose of plant cooling. From a management perspective, syringing a turf that is under a moisture stress (wilting) has a positive effect on reducing canopy temperatures (i.e., supplying the plant/soil with moisture for transpiration). (Duff and Beard, 1966) However, where moisture is not limiting, syringing should have a minimal effect on cooling the turf. (DiPaola, 1984) For example, on cloudy hot days with little air movement and high humidity, syringing has little effect.

Plant recovery from chronic temperature stress begins with fall fertilization. As the days become shorter and the weather cooler, grasses slow their vertical growth and begin to grow laterally. At the same time, carbohydrates that were depleted during the summer are now being accumulated and stored. Nitrogen provides the necessary nutrition to promote carbohydrate formation.

DORMANCY

Dormancy is one of the important mechanisms nature has devised to help plants survive stressful conditions. Dormancy can occur in response to moisture deficits and high temperatures (summer) or in response to cold temperatures (winter). Summer dormancy in cool-season turfgrasses results in senescence of the plant's leaves and stems, and the inactivation of crown buds. In winter dormancy, the buds are inactive but the crowns, rhizomes and stolons are still actively growing. Summer dormancy was described previously (Chapter 4) while winter dormancy, as governed by temperature, is the focus here.

The highest level of dormancy is termed true dormancy and is defined as the point in which a plant, if exposed to favorable conditions, will not immediately resume growth. (Vegis, 1964) Lesser levels of dormancy can occur in turfgrasses, especially cool-season turfgrasses, which are more aptly described as resting or quiescence stages. Turfgrass in a quiescent stage of dormancy quickly resumes growth with the onset of favorable growing conditions.

The stage of dormancy regarding warm-season turfgrasses depends on the climatic conditions. Bermudagrass may never go into dormancy when grown in a tropical climate such as south Florida. As you move farther north into colder winters, bermudagrass may reach a stage of true dormancy. At this point, if temperatures rise above freezing, dormancy is not broken. To the southern turfgrass manager this physiological shutdown of the plant allows for the potential use of herbicides such as glyphosate and paraquat for weed control on dormant bermudagrass. These types of herbicides could not be used on actively growing bermudagrass without causing serious injury or death.

Factors that can interact with temperature to induce winter dormancy are: light, photoperiod, nutritional level and moisture. Light intensities are important especially in breaking dormancy. Light is required for photosynthesis which supplies the

Injury caused by mowing during a period of high temperature and low moisture levels. The damage around the perimeter of the green is a result of mowing the cleanup pass.

energy needed for plant growth. The role photoperiod plays in dormancy has not been fully investigated, although it is believed to be minor. However, why some cultivars of a turfgrass species go dormant sooner than others or resume growth later in the spring might be linked to photoperiod. Photoperiod in a number of plants is an important factor in inducing dormancy. In some deciduous trees the initiation of short days triggers dormancy while longer days (spring) can be responsible for breaking dormancy. The lack of moisture and nutrition, primarily nitrogen, can bring about dormancy sooner than expected. In areas where warm-season turfgrasses are overseeded with a cool-season turfgrass, managers often try to promote dormancy in warm-season grasses by withholding water and nitrogen weeks before overseeding the turf. This is done to minimize any competition from the warm-season grasses to the overseeded cool-season grasses.

Chilling injury is generally associated with warm-season turfgrasses. Once the temperature drops to around 50 F, water uptake and retention can be obstructed causing the plants to discolor. Physiological responses may include disruption of photosynthesis, respiration and carbohydrate partitioning. (White and Schmidt, 1989) Attempts at extending the greening period through chilling conditions with growth hormone applications have had mixed success. Applications of gibberellic acid have improved color on bermudagrass, but increased chilling injury on St. Augustinegrass. (Karnok and Beard, 1983) Although not a growth hormone, iron applications during the growing season appear to extend the greening period of bermudagrass into the fall without adversely affecting the breaking of dormancy in the spring. (White and Schmidt, 1990)

Although chilling injury is normally associated with warm-season turfgrasses, it has been reported to occur on cool-season turfgrasses. A one-day chilling temperature of 46 F and night temperature of 41 F resulted in a photosynthetic reduction of 85 percent to 90 percent in perennial ryegrass. Full photosynthetic activity did not occur until after seven days of 72 F day temperatures and 63 F night temperatures. (Moon et al, 1990)

Cold-hardiness is the ability of a turfgrass plant to survive suboptimal temperatures. Turfgrass plants acquire cold-hardiness by exposure to successively lower temperatures. Turfgrasses begin to acclimate to cold temperatures in July and August, and the acclimation process steadily increases through January. (White and Smithberg, 1980) Maximum cold-hardiness of both cold- and warm-season turfgrasses occurs during early to midwinter. (December to January) Leaves are the most cold-tolerant part of the plant with survival occurring as low as - 40 F. (Gusta et al, 1980)

Crowns, stolons and rhizomes are less cold-tolerant than leaves. However, the cold hardiness of crowns, stolons and rhizomes is of greater concern because new growth initiates from these plant parts.

Physiologically, the degree of hardiness in plants is stated simply as "those plants able to tolerate more of their water being frozen." (Burke et al, 1976) When internal plant temperatures drop below freezing, ice crystals begin to form in the extracellular spaces with water from the cells diffusing out of the cell toward the ice crystals. In cold-hardy (frost) plants, once the water melts the water diffuses back into the cell and metabolism begins. In non-acclimated or frost-sensitive plants, the melted water does not completely return to the cell and metabolism does not resume. Plants are most susceptible to cold damage during the acclimation phase in the fall and the deacclimation stage in late winter to early spring.

The deacclimation stage is the most critical to turfgrass survival. (Beard, 1966; White and Smithberg, 1980) Once deacclimation is initiated, the turfgrass plant's cold hardiness is lost and cannot be regained with exposure to cold temperatures. (Gusta et al, 1980) During late winter and early spring the growing points are beginning to rehydrate and are susceptible to periods of internal freezing and thawing. Management practices such as soil drainage that removes excess water away from the turfgrass crown during late winter and early spring may minimize external freezing and thawing cycles. During these freezing and thawing cycles, traffic should be minimized on wet turfs.

Cool-season turfgrasses are more cold-hardy than warm-season turfgrasses. Cool-season turfgrasses withstand cold temperatures from 5 to - 17 F with some reports of Kentucky bluegrass and creeping bentgrass surviving at temperatures as low as -55 F. (White and Smithberg, 1980) Warm-season turfgrasses are less tolerant to cold than cool-season grasses which have a cold temperature tolerance ranging from 23 F to - 10 F. Except for buffalograss and blue gama, most warm-season grasses have a cold temperature tolerance above freezing. (Table 1)

Differences in cold hardiness among cultivars of a species exist. For example within the chewing fescues, the cultivars "Atlanta," "Highlight" and "Wintergreen" have killing temperatures of 0, -5 and -17 F, respectively. (Rajashekar et al, 1983)

Turfgrass plants are most resistant to cold temperatures during December and January.

TEMPERATURE AS A PREDICTIVE INSTRUMENT

As previously mentioned, temperature influences plant growth and development. Temperature fluctuations are not restricted just to plants, however; it also influences the growth and development of organisms which do not regulate internal temperatures (cold-blooded). The development of whole plants and organisms shows a temperature response due to the many individual physiological events affected by temperature. Generally, organism development occurs at a greater rate at higher temperatures than at lower temperatures. Most organisms have a minimum temperature where growth will occur and an upper temperature where growth ceases. A relationship exists with a number of organisms between growth and development and an accumulation of temperature. The accumulation of temperature over time may be related to developmental responses in organisms. Growing degree-day (GDD) is a means of quantifying seasonal accumulation of temperature and is commonly expressed as:

$$GDD = \frac{\text{maximum} + \text{minimum daily temperature}}{2} - \text{base temperature}$$

where the (maximum + minimum daily temperature)/2 equals the average daily temperature, and the base temperature represents the minimum temperature needed for growth. Base temperature for growth is dependent on the organism. However, a commonly used base temperature is 50 degrees F. Degree-days are calculated daily and are accumulated from a starting date which is often the first of January. An example of calculating growing degree-days is provided in Table 2. If a GDD calculation yields zero or a negative number, then zero GDDs occurred for that day.

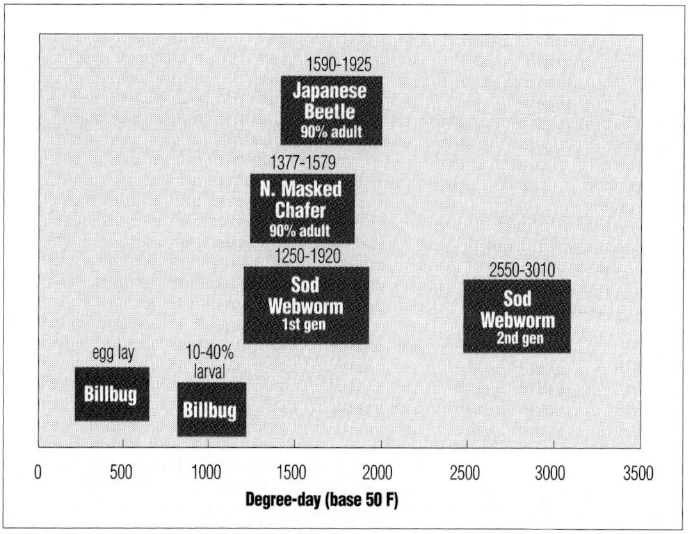

Figure 4. The development stages of a select number of insect pests based on growing degree-days. (Shetlar, 1991) (gen = generation)

The accumulation of GDDs are then associated with organism developmental stages. Examples of models using GDD for predicting turfgrass growth and turf insect pests are listed in Table 3. Turfgrass managers can or will be able to use GDD models to predict plant flowering, rooting, weed emergence and insect development. Pest control measures based on GDD models may provide an efficient and timely means for basing pesticide applications. In Figure 4, for example, the timing of an insecticide for adult control of the bluegrass billbug is targeted between 200 and 500 GDD. Another example is the use of GDD models for suppressing the flowering of certain turfgrass plants with plant growth regulators. (Branham and Danneberger, 1989) Subsequently, advantages gained by using GDD models for the variability of basing chemical applications on a calendar date is eliminated. Applications are instead based on the organism's growth and not an arbitrary date.

Sensitivity of Warm-Season Turfgrasses to Cold Temperatures

Relative Cold Tolerance	Warm-season Turfgrass[F]	Relative Killing Temperature (F)	Cool-season Turfgrass	Relative Killing Temperature (F)
Excellent	Buffalograss	-10	Creeping Bentgrass[B]	-5 to -10
	Blue gama	-10	Chewings Fescue[R]	0 to -17
			Kentucky Bluegrass[R]	-1 to -8
			Red Fescue[R]	-5
Very Good	Zoysiagrass	6		
Good	Bermudagrass	19	Perennial Ryegrass[BR]	5 to -3
			Annual Bluegrass[B]	5
Poor	Centipedegrass	11	Tall Fescue[B]	15
	Seashore Paspalum	19		
Very Poor	St. Augustinegrass	23	Annual Ryegrass[B]	25
	Bahiagrass	23		
	Carpetgrass	23		

TABLE 1.

[B] data from: Beard, J.B. 1966. Michigan Quarterly Bulletin 48(3):377-383.
[F] data from: Frey, J. 1991. *Lawn & Landscape Maintenance* 12:26-29.
[R] data from: Rajashekar, C., D. Tao and P.H. Li. 1983. HortScience 18:91-93.

Example of Calculating Growing Degree-Days Using a Base Temperature of 50 F

Date	Maximum Daily Temperature (F)	Minimum Daily Temperature (F)	Accumulated Growing Degree-day units[#]	Accumulated Growing Degree-day units
January 1	40	20	0	0
*	*	*	*	*
*	*	*	*	*
March 1	50	30	0	0
March 2	60	40	0	0
March 3	66	50	8	8
March 4	70	54	12	20
March 5	60	40	0	20
March 6	60	50	5	25
*	*	*	*	*
*	*	*	*	*

TABLE 2.   [#] GDD = average daily temperature [(maximum + minimum)/2] minus base temperature

Proposed Models for Turfgrass Growth and Insect Development Using Growing Degree-Days

Turfgrass/Insect	Description	Citation
Annual Bluegrass	predicts seedhead emergence	Danneberger, T.K. and J.M. Vargas Jr. 1984 Agronomy Journal 76:756-758.
Annual Bluegrass	predicts temperature stress periods	Danneberger, T.K. and J.R. Street. 1985. Ohio J. Sci. 85:108-111.
Cool-Season Turfs	predicts temperature stress periods	Danneberger, T.K. and A.J. Turgeon. 1985. V Inter. Turfgrass Conf. 5:802-806.
Kentucky Bluegrass	predicts root growth	Koski, A.J., J.R. Street and T.K. Danneberger. 1988. Crop Science 28:848-850.
Tall Fescue	predicts seedhead emergence	DiPaola, J.M., W.M. Lewis and W.B. Gilbert. 1987. Agronomy Abstr. 13.
Chinchbug	predicts life cycle	Lin, H.J. and F.L. McEwen. 1979. Environ. Entomology 8: 512-515.
Sod Webworm	predicts life cycle	Tolley, M.P. 1986. Journal Economical Entomology 79:400-404.
Fruit Fly	predicts life cycle	Tolley, M.P. and H.D. Niemczyk. 1988. Journal Economical Entomology 81: 1346-1351.

TABLE 3.

6

Soil: Ecology's Anchor

The nation that destroys its soil destroys itself.
— Franklin D. Roosevelt, U.S. president

THE COMPOSITION and characteristics of soil influence how turfgrass plants grow and develop by providing nutrient, water and physical support. Soil properties define the environmental conditions for organism interaction and survival, making soil the anchor to the study of turfgrass ecology.

The properties of soil make it both a resource and a condition. As a resource, soil properties determine the availability of moisture for plant growth and, through inherent chemical properties, govern the retention of nutrients. As a condition soil compaction, soil aeration, soil pH and the presence of toxic substances influence the distribution and survival of turfgrass plants and organisms.

THE SOIL PROFILE

Soils develop at the Earth's surface through chemical weathering and biological activity. From these processes, distinct soil layers or horizons develop. In a typical soil profile four major horizons develop termed the O, A, B and C horizons. (Figure 1) The O horizon is an organic or litter layer that forms above the soil. This layer primarily occurs in forest soils rather than turfgrass soils. However, on intensively managed turf, a thatch layer will develop similar to an O horizon.

Thatch is defined as a layer of living and dead stems, roots and crowns that develops between green vegetation and the soil surface. Excessive thatch is associated with detrimental turf effects and can be the cause of wide temperature and moisture fluctuations, providing a habitat for certain pests, reduced efficacy of certain pesticides, nutrient availability and a reduction in seedling viability in renovated turfs.

The A horizon develops at or near the soil surface and is often referred to as topsoil. It is the darkest of the horizons and may vary in depth from a couple of inches to more than a foot. In grass situations, the darker color of the A horizon comes from profuse root production and high organic content. This horizon is the

75

richest in available nutrients for turfgrass growth.

The B horizon is a zone of maximum accumulation of clays and soil oxides. This horizon is sometimes referred to as the subsoil. In turfgrass soils, the B horizon often becomes the "topsoil" through construction modification. For example, home builders may invert the soil or scrape off the A horizon during foundation excavation exposing the B horizon. In these situations turfgrass will have to be maintained on the B horizon. As a zone of clay accumulation, turfgrasses established in this environment will be more prone to compaction and require greater fertilization due to the low organic matter content. The C horizon is unconsolidated material that lies beneath the soil and normally represents the parent material for the soil.

Soils are composed of four major components: soil solids (soil matrix), organic matter, air and water. (Figure 2) A desirable soil might be composed of 45 percent solids, 5 percent organic matter and 25 percent each of air and water.

SOIL SOLIDS

The solid phase of a soil is comprised of a mineral or inorganic component and an organic (organic matter). The inorganic portion of the soil may be separated into primary minerals and secondary minerals. A primary mineral has persisted over-time with little chemical change from its original parent material. A secondary mineral has undergone a weathering process which has chemically changed the features of the mineral from the original parent material. Secondary minerals formed by the weathering of less resistant minerals include iron oxides and silicate clays.

Three inorganic particles exist and are known as sand, soil and clay. Sand is predominantly quartz and is a primary mineral that varies in shape from round to angular. Of the three particles, sand is the largest ranging from 2 millimeters (mm) to 0.05 mm. Particles greater than 2 mm are often referred to as pebbles, gravel and stones. Sand is further classified into five particle size groups. (Table 1)

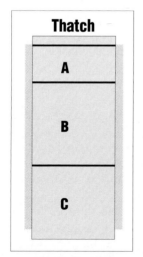

Figure 1. The soil profile.

Silt is intermediate in size between sand and clay with particle sizes ranging from 0.05 to 0.002 mm. Silt, as with sand, is composed primarily of quartz (primary mineral) with some iron and aluminum oxides (secondary mineral). Silt is similar to fine sand since it is chemically inert. Clay has the smallest particle size of the inorganic soil solids. Through weathering processes, clay is chemically altered from the parent material. Thus, clays are considered secondary minerals.

SOIL TEXTURE

The percentage by weight of the sand, silt and clay particles determines the texture of the soil. (Figure 3) For example, a soil having 40 percent sand, 40 percent silt and 20 percent clay will intersect in the loam region. It is interesting to note that a relatively small percentage of clay can cause a texture to be classified in some manner as a clay. For a soil to be sandy, however, a large portion of the soil must be sand. This point is often forgotten by turf managers who attempt to modify a soil by the addition of small quantities of sand.

Sandy soils contribute little to the water holding capacity of a soil. Total sand porosity is small, but the individual pore sizes are large. These large pores allow water to move rapidly through the soil providing drainage. In general, sands are resistant to compaction and the cation exchange capacity of sand is low resulting in poor nutrient retention.

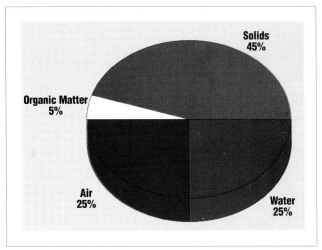

Figure 2. The four components of soil.

Soils with high silt content retain water better than sands, and a large portion of the retained water is available for plant growth. Pores from silt are smaller than those from sand accounting for greater water retention, but are larger than clay which makes a greater amount of water available for plant growth. The susceptibility of silt to compaction is great and water drainage is intermediate between sand and clay.

Clay soils have a higher porosity than either sand or silt due to their greater number of pores. However, the pore sizes are so small that the actual amount of water available for plant growth is small because of the tenacity by which water is held. (See soil moisture.) Clay is susceptible to compaction and slow to drain. Clay particles are chemically active accounting for most of the nutrient retention of a soil.

Soil colloids are clay particles and an organic fraction (humus) with sizes less than 1 micron (0.001 mm). Col-

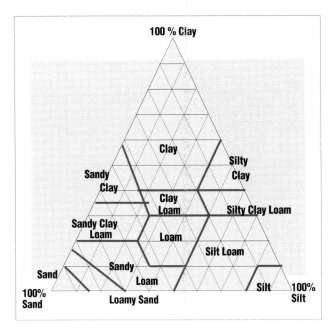

Figure 3. The textural triangle.

loids account for a large portion of the soil's chemical activity. The colloidal fraction carries both a negative and positive charge. The negative charge is often of greater importance since it attracts and retains cationic plant nutrients for later plant uptake. The ability of these colloids to retain cations is expressed as cation exchange capacity (CEC). Cation exchange capacity is defined as milliequivalent (me) per 100 grams of oven dry soil. The usefulness of CEC is to give an estimate of the nutrient retention capacity of the soil. Soil CEC values can range from as low as 2 to in excess of 180 me/100 grams on high organic content soils.

SOIL AGGREGATION

In soils containing substantial amounts of clay and/or silt, the individual soil particles clump or aggregate together to form larger units. Soil aggregation often results in the development of larger inter-aggregate pores big enough to hold water for plant growth and provide adequate drainage through the soil profile. For example, if silt and clay are present in the soil as separate particles with no aggregation, intermixing would result in a soil with many small pores, one that is susceptible to compaction and a soil with low plant water availability.

Aggregation produces large pore spaces between aggregates resulting in better plant growth and drainage. Soil aggregation is enhanced through alternating cycles of wetting and drying and freezing and thawing, together with root growth and the mixing activity of soil organisms. Soil aggregates, along with soil particles, determine the soil structure. Generally, four types of soil structures exist: platelike, prismlike, blocklike and spheroidal. Platelike structures can occur anywhere in the profile and is evidence of compaction. Prismlike arrangements are found in arid and semiarid regions, and blocklike structures are common in subsoils with high clay contents. Spheroidal or granular structures are common at or near the soil surface and is the preferred condition for plant growth.

Important in the stability of aggregates is the degree of organic interaction with the particles. Microbial and organic matter (humus) interactions causes the cementing of aggregates which in turn results in greater stability. In turf situations where soils are high in silts and clays, the addition of an organic source such as peat promotes soil aggregation. Since sands tend not to aggregate, a uniform sand particle size is desirable.

A soil profile showing a thatch layer between the green vegetation and the soil. Note that another layer had developed further down in the soil profile. In this situation, a homeowner buried the original turf with soil and then overseeded creating a new turf.

SOIL MOISTURE

The spaces between soil particles are called pores. These pores hold both the water and air necessary for plant

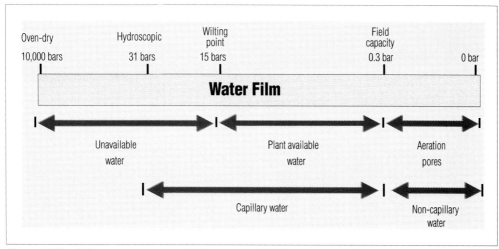

Figure 4. The different tensions at which water is held in a soil particle.

growth. (The air component of soils was previously mentioned in Chapter 3.) Classifying soil water is based on how tightly it is held. Water that drains freely through the soil is termed gravitational water and is unavailable for plant growth. In a saturated soil where water is flowing freely, the pores that drain first are the large pores called macropores. Macropores, once drained, are filled with air providing a necessary element for healthy turfgrass development. A uniform, medium to coarse sand is characterized by having a large number of macropores.

Once gravitational water has drained, the remaining water in the soil is called soil moisture. Water is held in soil pores through capillary action. Capillary action functions through the adhesion of water to the soil particle and the cohesion between adjacent water molecules. The portion of the capillary water that is held tightly in small pores — unavailable to the plant — is referred to as unavailable water. The portion of water that is not gravitational and can be taken up by the plant is called plant available water.

The total water holding capacity of a soil can be subdivided by determining how tightly the water, measured in bars, is held to the surface of the soil particles. (Figure 4) Plant available water is defined as water held by the soil between field capacity, which is the point where gravitational flow stops (1/3 bar) and the permanent wilting point where water is held so tightly that it is unavailable for plant growth (15 bars). At 31 bars, water is held so tightly that capillary movement no longer occurs. Beyond 31 bars, removal of water from the soil can only be accomplished by oven drying (221 F). The amount of available soil moisture present for plant growth varies depending on the soil texture. (Figure 5) Coarse-textured soils hold less water between field capacity and the wilting point than fine-textured soils. However, very fine-textured soils do not hold much plant available water due to the large amount of unavailable water.

Capillary water flow is dependent on soil texture and soil compaction. Capillary

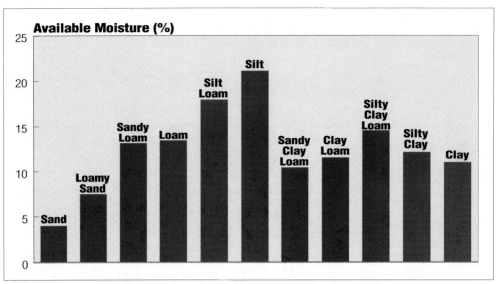

Figure 5. Plant available moisture for the 12 textural classes. (Waddington, 1969)

water flow occurs through water filled pores and the thin films of water around soil particles. Resistance to water flow occurs with a textural change in the soil profile. If a coarse-textured soil lies on top of a fine-textured soil, the speed at which the water moves through the coarse-textured material is slowed markedly when it reaches the finer-textured soil. This stoppage of water flow results in a perched water table.

Additionally, if a fine-textured soil lies on top of a coarse-textured soil, water flow through the fine-textured soil will be delayed until a sufficient ponding of water is created in this layer to force its way into the coarse-textured layer below. This also creates a perched water table in the fine-textured layer. The concept of a perched water table in this second situation is useful in the construction of golf greens and athletic fields. A deep uniform sand topmix is too droughty to support plant growth due to the small amount of soil moisture. However, by placing a sandy topmix over a coarse-textured material, water can be perched in the sandy topmix to provide moisture for plant growth.

As mentioned before, capillary water flow is restricted when a fine-textured soil lies on top of a coarse-textured soil. In this case, points of water contact between the two textures is minimal. Until water accumulates in the finer-textured soil to a point where it can break through the boundary, no downward water movement occurs. Once water flows into the coarser material, rapid movement occurs.

SOIL COMPACTION

Turfgrass growth promotes beneficial soil aggregation and permeability. However, foot traffic often counteracts the beneficial aspects of turf growth by causing compaction. Compaction is the result of soil aggregates and particles being packed closely together. Compacted soils have increased bulk density,* and a reduction in the number of large pores that contain air. (Canaway, 1978) A decrease in the number of large pores with a corresponding increase in the number of small pores causes a reduction in water infiltration rates.

The susceptibility of a soil to compaction increases as soil moisture increases to field capacity. At some critical soil moisture content (generally near field capacity), a point of maximum compaction for a given surface occurs. Beyond this point the addition of water does not increase compaction because many of the pores are now filled with water which is incompressible. Compacted soils conduct heat to a greater extent than more porous and better aerated soils. This is due to the many water filled pores that are in contact with each other. In addition, as a result of the many small water filled pores compacted soils require more heat to raise the soil temperature. From a management perspective, wet compacted soils in the spring are cool which can delay seed germination.

Compaction changes pore size distribution by reducing the number of large pores which in turn causes a reduction in both water infiltration and percolation rates. On heavily trafficked turfs such as athletic fields and golf course putting greens, reduced infiltration and percolation rates can cause a deterioration in the playing surfaces. The texture of a soil can influence its tendency to compaction. Typically, silty soils are more prone to compaction because of its relatively fine texture and weak aggregates. Clay, while fine-textured, tends to have stronger aggregates that are more resistant to compaction. Sands are the most resistant of the soil particles to compaction because the particles are resistant to pressures that might mold them into different shapes.

MODIFIED SOIL MIXES

In high traffic situations, modified soil mixes containing a large percentage of sand are used to reduce the potential for compaction. Sand, as previously mentioned, is resistant to compaction and promotes rapid infiltration and percolation rates. Soil mixes used in high traffic areas should have at least 90 percent sand in the mix. (Baker, 1988; Taylor and Blake, 1979) Mixes containing less than 90 percent sand do not have adequate infiltration rates and in some instances result in surface ponding of water. (Baker, 1988) However, even on 100 percent sand mixes, traffic can reduce infiltration rates. To retard the decline in infiltration rates on 100 percent sand mixes, aeration followed by sand topdressing should be practiced. (Baker, 1988)

In some instances an organic source, primarily peat, is added to enhance moisture and nutrient retention in high sand mixes, but standards to judge the quality of peat for mixes is lacking. Thus, deciding on the proper peat depends on the experience of the user or the testing laboratory. Recent work with peat for rootzone mixes has found that the peat source should exceed 80 percent organic matter by weight, be neither too coarse nor too fine and have fiber contents between 20 percent and 45 percent. (McCoy, 1992)

In addition, when the sand and peat is combined, the final mix should not exceed

---

Bulk density is the mass (weight) of soil per given volume of dry soil. The units are given as g/cc where g = grams and cc = cubic centimeters.

3 percent to 4 percent organic matter by weight. A ranking of peats from excellent to poor are: peat humus, reed-sedge peat, hypnum moss peat and sphagnum moss peat. (Beard, 1982) However, much variation in fiber content can occur within these different types of peat. Consequently, when choosing a peat it is best to judge the quality of the peat on its fiber and organic content.

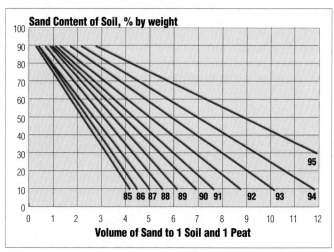

Figure 6. Calculating the amount of sand needed in a sand: soil:peat mix. Critical factor in determining the amount of sand is knowing the soil that is being used. (See text for explanation.)

The introduction of soil into a topmix for the purpose of enhancing nutrient and moisture retention can cause significant mix variations. If a mix contained a soil with high sand content, the performance would be considerably different than a mix with a soil component high in clay. The mix high in clay is more susceptible to compaction than the one containing predominantly sand.

Taylor and Blake (1984) proposed a means for achieving a desired sand:soil:peat mix. By analyzing the soil to determine the amount of sand in that soil one could achieve a desired sand level in the mix by combining sand with a soil:peat base. For example in Figure 6, if you wanted to end up with a sand:soil:peat mix containing 87 percent sand, you would have to determine the percent sand in the soil. (For this example, 30 percent will be used.) Now, by determining where the two lines intersect, the amount of sand needed for each unit of soil and peat is given as four loads of sand for every one of soil and peat. Caution should be used when following this approach to making a mix because the "quality" of the sand in the soil fraction is unknown and you may end up contaminating a high quality sand with a low quality sand from the soil.

EFFECTS OF COMPACTION ON TURFGRASS GROWTH

As previously mentioned, compacted soils in turfgrass situations often occur under high traffic conditions. Although compaction and wear from traffic can occur together, turfgrass plant responses are different. Wear is the physical abrasion and tearing of above ground plant parts (Beard, 1973), while compaction influences bulk density, water relations and pore size distribution.

Turfgrasses growing on compacted soils have reduced overall visual quality, less tillering and leaf growth, shallower root systems, lower evapotranspiration rates and lower nitrogen use. Compacted soils impede and restrict root and stem growth by acting as a physical barrier to root penetration. Kentucky bluegrass cultivars grown on compacted soils displayed restricted stem development and increased incidence to disease. (Shearman and Watkins, 1985) From a competitive standpoint, no differences in stem growth between Kentucky bluegrass cultivars occurred. However, the response of species to compaction varies. Cool-season turfgrasses such as perennial ryegrass and Kentucky bluegrass have better tolerance to compaction than tall fescue. (Carrow, 1980) Attempts to compensate for the effects of compaction — primarily a reduction in turfgrass growth — by the addition of nitrogen have had no effect. (Sills and Carrow, 1983) Actually, high nitrogen rates together with compaction, greatly restricts root growth.

Wear tolerance is the ability of turfgrasses to withstand the process of wear. (Canaway, 1983) Wear can cause compaction and is reflected in increased bulk density and decreased pore space. Yet, wear does not necessarily lead to compaction. (Canaway, 1981) Wear tolerance is easily judged by visual rating systems and by the percent of plant cover remaining after the treatment. (Shearman and Beard, 1975a) Turfgrass plants that have a high percentage of sclerenchyma fibers and lignified cells are closely associated with wear tolerance. (Shearman and Beard, 1975b) However, the use of sclerified and lignified cells as a measure of wear tolerance does not appear to be a good indication when looking at a number of turfgrasses. (Canaway, 1978)

Wear tolerance of cool-season grasses as measured by percent cover and biomass production is as follows: *Poa annua* > *Lolium perenne* > *Poa pratensis* > *Festuca arundinacea* > *Festuca rubra spp. commutata* > *Festuca rubra spp. rubra.* (Canaway,1983) Although *poa annua* has good wear tolerance other playing factors such as shear strength, which is the ability of the soil and turf to withstand both vertical and horizontal forces (slippage), make it a poor turf for athletic fields. For use on athletic fields, perennial ryegrass is suitable. Kentucky bluegrass is also suitable but lacks persistence. Tall fescue is not as good, and fine fescues are unsuitable for use. (Canaway, 1983)

MECHANICAL PRACTICES FOR REDUCING COMPACTION

Reducing compaction through the installation of a modified topmix in large turf areas may not be practical. A number of mechanical means to reduce compaction are available, including core cultivation, slicing and spiking. Core cultivation increases the number of macropores in the upper layers of the soil profile. Traditional coring is done to a 2 1/2- to 3-inch depth with either spoons or tines. Spoons enter and exit the soil in a wide arc resulting in the removal of a soil core and loosening of the soil. Spoons are more commonly used in residential turfgrass situations and on some golf course fairways.

Hollow tines are inserted vertically (up and down motion) into the soil causing the removal of a soil core. If the removed core is brushed back into the hole created by coring, it will be less compacted. Alternatively, the core can be removed and the holes left open or filled with a topdressing material. Core cultivation with hollow tines causes disruption to the turf surface, but not to the same degree as spoons. Solid

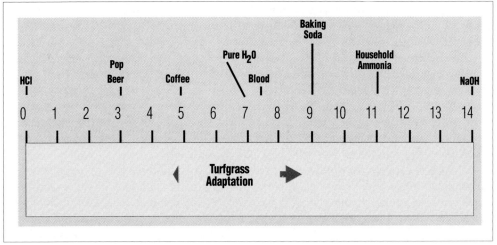

Figure 7. pH scale showing the range of turfgrass adaptation. As a benchmark, pHs of common products, blood and water are provided.

tines have been used to reduce compaction and cause less disturbance to the turfgrass surface. Both hollow and solid tines produce macropores, but hollow tines provide aeration to a greater degree. (Murphy and Rieke, 1991)

Tines may produce a cultivation pan if coring is done consistently to the same depth. The likelihood of a cultivation pan is greatest under wet conditions and with the use of solid tines. (Murphy et al, 1993) If the cultivation pan becomes a significant problem deep tine cultivation may be required.

A new method of relieving compaction is the use of high pressure water injection to penetrate and shatter the soil. High pressure water injection significantly increases water infiltration rates to a deeper depth than traditional coring with little turf disturbance.

Slicing produces deep vertical cuts, but the soil is not extracted. This practice may give temporary relief to compaction, but the lack of soil removal and the pressing of soil particles closer together around the slicing blade may cause localized compaction. Spiking is similar to slicing but is not done to the same depth.

Spiking may temporarily relieve crusting which is caused by water hitting the soil and dispersing fine soil particles into surface pores. The clogging of pores makes the surface susceptible to compaction and reduces any water flow into the soil. Spiking is used most frequently on putting greens to stimulate plant growth through the severing of stems.

pH

pH influences the distribution and abundance of organisms in a soil. pH characterizes soils as either acid or basic. The pH scale ranges from 1 to 14 with 7 being neutral. Values less than 7 are acid and values greater than 7 are considered alkaline. (Figure 7) Soils vary in their pH values. For example, bog soils containing sulfur will range in pH from 1 to 3; humid forest soils will range in pH from 4 to 6.5; subhumid grassland soils will range from 5 to 7; and semiarid grassland soils will range in pH from 6.5 to 8.

pH influences the decomposition rate of organic matter. Bacteria decomposers are not as tolerant to acid soil conditions as fungi. The effects of pH on organic matter accumulation and decomposition is further discussed under soil organic matter.

In acid soils with pH values less than 5, a high concentration of aluminum ions occurs which is extremely toxic to plants. On highly basic soils — such as alkaline soils — iron, magnesium and phosphate become unavailable for plant growth. Most turfgrass plants are best adapted to a pH range of 5.5 to 7.8. Some turfgrasses such as zoysiagrass, centipedegrass and carpetgrass are somewhat tolerant to pHs below 5.0.

pH influences the health of turfgrass plants and their competitive ability by determining the resource (nutrient) availability. (Table 2) The ideal pH for plant growth is 6.5 because the nutrients needed for growth are in a form that is plant available. As the pH becomes more acidic or basic, some nutrients become less available.

SPECIAL SOIL SITUATIONS

Calcareous soils or sands are characterized by having high amounts of calcium carbonate ($CaCO_3$). Calcareous soils are easily detected by the addition of 10 percent hydrochloric acid (HCl). The hydrochloric acid reacts with the calcium carbonate causing a bubbling which is the result of CO_2 evolution. Effervescence is the term used to describe the reaction of 10 percent HCl with soils. The alkaline pH of calcareous sands is caused by the hydrolysis

Calcium deposits on a newly seeded turf caused by irrigation with a calcareous water source.

of $CaCO_3$ to form calcium hydroxide ($CaOH_2$) a strong base, and carbonic acid (H_2CO_3) a weak acid.

A strong base dissociates more readily producing more OH^- ions than the H^+ ions produced from the dissociation of a weak acid. Calcareous soils may have a pH as high as 8.3. If calcareous sands are used in a rootzone mix, attempts to lower the soil pH with the addition of sulfur to the surface will result in a dissolution of the $CaCO_3$. This dissolved $CaCO_3$ will leach through the profile and precipitate at a lower, high pH zone. Over time, this precipitation of $CaCO_3$ will build up a low permeability pan in the rootzone. (McCoy, personal communication)

Saline soils contain enough soluble salts to impair turfgrass growth. Due to the soluble salt concentration, the conductivity of these soils exceeds 4 millimhos/cm. (See Chapter 4, for turfgrasses adapted to these conditions.) The major cations present are magnesium, calcium and sodium. Sodium makes up less than 15 percent of the soluble cations that are present in saline soils. Compared to sodic soils, defined below, saline soils can still have good structure. A symptom of saline soils is the accumulation of a white crust on the soil surface and a pH value of 8.5 or less. Correcting saline conditions consists of leaching the salts out of the profile with water. Success requires a good subsurface drainage system below the root system to remove the salts from the site and minimize the concentration of salts in the rootzone.

Sodic soils differ from saline soils in its sodium content and its affects on soil structure. Sodic soils are non-saline soils that contain large amounts of sodium with a sodium absorption ratio of 15 or more. The high sodium content causes a dispersion of soil particles and poor soil structure. This dispersion causes the soil to be impermeable to water. The combination of high sodium and the dispersed nature of the soil makes turfgrass growth difficult. Gypsum ($CaSO_4$) is used on high so-

Core cultivation with hollow tines is a common turfgrass management practice to relieve compaction. (Bottom photo courtesy of Mark Yoder)

dium soils to improve soil structure. When gypsum is added to a sodic soil, the calcium replaces the sodium which in turn is leached from the soil resulting in improved soil structure.

Hydrophobic soils are soils that resist wetting. The condition associated with a hydrophobic soil and a turfgrass species is referred to as localized dry spots. Localized dry spots result in drought stress to the plant community due to the presence of water repellant substances. Localized dry spots are most often associated with sandy soils. However, localized dry spots are frequently observed on native soils. The hydrophobic soil condition is generally attributed to a difference in soil organic matter coating the soil particles. The classes of soil organic matter that are most frequently associated with hydrophobic soils include lipids, proteinaceous compounds, humic acid, fulvic acids, lignin and suberin. Fungi have been implicated in the development of hydrophobic soils by directly causing or influencing soil structure and aggregate stability. (Hudson, 1992)

SOIL ORGANIC MATTER
Soil organisms decompose plant residues into an enormous array of organic compounds in various states of decomposition. The most decomposed state is

humus which is resistant to further decomposition. Although organic matter is not a mineral soil particle like sand, silt or clay, it significantly contributes to the properties of a soil. Humus provides the soil with increased nutrient retention through its high cation exchange capacity (see soil colloids), increased water holding capabilities and a source of nitrogen for plant growth.

THATCH

Thatch is composed of intact roots, nodes of crowns and sclerified vascular strands of stems and leaf sheaths which are resistant to decay. (Ledeboer and Skogley, 1967) Thatch develops when plants are producing organic material at a greater rate than the decomposition rate. Any management practice that increases plant growth or decreases the decomposition rate contributes to thatch formation.

The four major management practices that contribute to thatch include: grass species, mowing, fertilization, pesticides and soil pH. Turfgrasses that are aggressively forming extensive root systems and stems (rhizomes and/or stolons) will thatch to a greater extent than turfgrasses lacking an extensive root and stem system. Turfgrasses such as bermudagrass, St. Augustinegrass and Kentucky bluegrass are more likely to produce thatch at a greater rate than perennial ryegrass, tall fescue and annual bluegrass. In addition, cultivar differences in vegetative growth influence thatch accumulation. (Shearman et al, 1983, 1986) From a management perspective, consideration should be given to cultivars that tend to thatch the least. Wear is a mitigating force in thatch formation which tends to counteract vegetative growth. (Shildrick, 1985)

Cultural practices such as mowing and nitrogen fertilization affect thatch accumulation. Mowing at heights that promote extensive root and/or stem development will thatch more readily than the same turf mowed at a much shorter height. High nitrogen applications have been associated with thatch accumulation. (Meinhold et al, 1973) Nitrogen, like establishing an aggressive turfgrass species or mowing at an optimum height, may promote thatch formation through increasing vegetative growth. In addition, acidifying nitrogen fertilizers may enhance thatch accumulation by reducing the soil pH which may inhibit microbial activity and earthworm populations. (Potter et al, 1985)

The use of certain pesticides on turf has had a profound effect on thatch accumulation. The applications of dieldrin, chlordane, bandane and calcium arsenate have been associated with excessive thatch accumulation. (Randell et al, 1972; Turgeon et al, 1975) In these studies a lack of earthworm activity was mentioned as a possible reason for excessive thatch formation. Certain fungicides such as benomyl, cadmium succinate, fenamiphos, iprodione and mancozeb have been associated with increased thatch accumulation. (Smiley et al, 1985) Thatch accumulation following fungicide applications does not appear to significantly alter the microbial population in the thatch or soil. (Smiley and Craven, 1979) Thus, fungicides appear to induce thatch by stimulating root and stem production and not by affecting the thatch decomposition rate. (Smiley et al, 1985)

Thatch has a low bulk density and is highly porous with generally large pore sizes. (Hurto et al, 1980). Thus, the pore sizes of thatch are analogous to sand. (Nelson et al, 1980) The physical properties of thatch cause disruption in capillary water flow from the thatch layer into the soil. The effect of thatch on infiltration rates is not much different than a soil with a coarse layer over a fine layer. If the thatch is initially dry, however, it can repel water and a significant reduction in infiltration rates can occur. (Taylor and Blake, 1982)

SOIL ORGANISMS — THE LIVING COMPONENT

The soil is teaming with diverse populations of living organisms. (Table 3) The vast majority of soil organisms live near the soil surface where the preponderance of soil organic material is present. Population levels drastically fall off as they move down into the B and C horizons. The greatest number of soil organisms are decomposers of organic residues. These small organisms, referred to as microorganisms, include bacteria, fungi, actinomycetes and algae. Soil microorganisms are important in the recycling of resources and energy such as carbon, nitrogen and sulfur; and in the transformational processes of nutrients such as iron and potassium. In the nitrogen cycle, microorganisms (primarily bacteria) break organic molecules into plant usable forms (mineralization), convert ammonia to nitrate and are involved in the processes of nitrogen fixation and denitrification. (See nitrogen cycle, Chapter 5.) The second group of soil organisms are the consumers of organic material. These organisms include the small animals such as earthworms and arthropods (i.e., mites, millipedes, centipedes, springtails).

Bacteria are usually the first to be present on dead organic material. Initially, bacteria use water soluble materials and sugars as an energy source. In turf, leaf clippings are composed of soluble materials that are rapidly decomposed. Microbial populations rapidly grow in the presence of these soluble sources. However, as soluble energy sources become less available microbial population growth slows. The slowing in microbial growth also reflects a slowing in the decomposition process because of the presence of complex molecules. Many of these bacteria do not have the necessary enzymes to digest complex molecules like lignin and cellulose.

Fungi play an important role in the degradation of these more complex molecules. The ability of fungi to decompose these molecules dictates the decomposition rate. Fungi are also very important in organic decomposition in acid soils since they are more tolerant to lower pH than bacteria. In addition, earthworms and arthropods consume plant residues and other organic matter fragments. These fragments are digested and then deposited through fecal material. Microorganisms are then able to readily break down the resultant smaller organic molecules.

As previously stated, thatch is a unique organic layer that is resistant to degradation. Similar to soil, thatch has a large microbial population. (Cole and Turgeon, 1978) Yet decomposition is slow because thatch is primarily vascular tissue containing few water-soluble compounds and more of the constituents including cellulose and lignin. (Ledeboer and Skogley, 1967) Attempts to introduce bacteria as thatch control agents is doomed to failure because of the lack of a bacterial enzyme system to degrade cellulose and lignin at any appreciable rate. Also, thatch is subject to extreme fluctuations in temperature and moisture, and may be nitrogen poor which can slow the decomposition rate.

However, fungi play a larger role in thatch decomposition. In a pot study, the introduction of the fungus *Phebia gigantea* significantly reduced the cellulose content in bermudagrass and centipedegrass thatch, while the fungus *Coriolus versicolor* significantly reduced the thatch lignin from a number of turfgrass species. (Sartain and Volk, 1984) Fungi appear to have specific metabolic processes. The rate of thatch decomposition is dependent on the presence of the proper species, adequate numbers of these decomposers and proper environmental conditions.

Soil animals that are of special interest are earthworms. A diversity of earthworm species exist which are important in the recycling of organic matter, nitrogen and phosphorus. Earthworms accelerate the decomposition and mineralization of organic matter by reducing the size of detritus particles available to microbes (Swift et al, 1979) or mineralizing nutrients directly (Syers et al, 1979). It is estimated from a tallgrass prairie in Kansas that 10 percent of the total soil organic matter in the top 6 inches pass through earthworms each year. (James, 1991) In turf, earthworms have been associated with enhancing thatch degradation by reducing the organic fragment particle size and mixing it with soil. Regarding nutrient cycling, earthworms process 10 percent to 12 percent of the mineral nitrogen plants take up yearly; and the phosphorus processed is equivalent to 50 percent of annual plant uptake. (James, 1991)

Earthworms affect soil physical structure through burrowing and casting. In turf, earthworm activity enhances infiltration rates of soils in the absence of traffic. (Baker, 1981) In the presence of traffic, however, broken down earthworm casts result in a surface layer of fine particle materials which are capable of clogging pores and increasing the potential for surface compaction. In addition, from an aesthetic point of view, earthworm casting may be disruptive to the overall desired smoothness of golf course putting greens or fairways. Certain pesticides are toxic to earthworms. Chapter 10 will discuss the effects of pesticides — both beneficial and detrimental — to plants and soil organisms.

Other soil animals work by ingesting organic material derived from either plants or other organisms, and through digestion and fecal passage provide materials more suitable for microbial decomposition. Destructive turfgrass insects such as grubs and nematodes can be thought of as decomposers. Grubs digest roots of turfgrass plants which are then digested and passed through for microbial decomposition. Nematodes parasitize plants, earthworms and other soil animals and injest decaying organic material. This consumption of plant or animal material, aids in its eventual decomposition. However, grub and nematode consumption of living organic materials causes a deleterious effect on the turfgrass plant.

Considerable numbers of turfgrass pathogens exist in the soil. The most prevalent pathogens are the fungi, with bacteria being present to a lesser degree. Soil pathogens are kept in check to some degree by disease suppressive microorganisms. In modified soils, microbial populations may be low and suppressive organisms may not be present. Gould (1973) observed that take-all patch was more prevalent on newly fumigated greens, a process where most if not all soil organisms are killed. However, as the turf matured take-all occurred with less frequency. Gould speculated that suppressive organisms where killed by fumigation and a period of time was needed for the suppressive organisms to re-establish. Researchers have identified disease suppressive (antagonistic) organisms to some common turfgrass pests. (Table 3)

In summary, soils are composed of the particles sand, silt and clay. The percentage of each particle determines the soil texture. The amount of soil water retained for plant growth is influenced by the texture and structure of the soil. Compaction caused by traffic is a serious problem in maintaining a healthy turfgrass community. Compaction can be relieved through soil modification by altering the particles in a topmix or through mechanical processes. And finally, organic matter decomposition is accomplished through a diverse soil population of microorganisms and soil animals. Each individual organism is not very versatile and depends on each other working together to decompose organic residuals.

Description and Comparison of the Different Particle Sizes

Particle	Diameter (mm)
Very Coarse Sand	1-2
Coarse Sand	1-0.5
Medium Sand	0.5-0.25
Fine Sand	0.25-0.10
Very Fine Sand	0.10-0.05
Silt	0.05-0.002
Clay	< 0.002

TABLE 1.

Estimate of Living Organisms in a Hectare of Soil to a Depth of 15 Centimeters in a Humid Temperate Region

Organism	Estimated Number of Individuals
Microorganisms	
Bacteria	2×10^{18}
Fungi	8×10^{16}
Actinomycetes	6×10^{17}
Algae	3×10^{14}
Protozoa	7×10^{16}
Non-arthropod animals	
Nematodes	2.5×10^{9}
Earthworms	7×10^{3}
Arthropod animals	
Springtails	4×10^{5}
Mites	4×10^{5}
Millipedes and centipedes	1×10^{3}
Harvestman (Opiliones)	2.5×10^{4}
Ants	5×10^{6}
Diplopoda, Chilopods, Symphyla	3.8×10^{7}
Diptera, Coleoptera, Lepidoptera	5×10^{7}
Vertebrate animals	
Mice, voles, moles	4×10^{5}
Rabbits, squirrels, gophers	10
Birds	100

TABLE 2.   *(Adapted with permission from Soil Genesis and Classification by S.W. Buol, F.D. Hole and R.J. McCracken. 1972. Iowa State University Press, Ames, Iowa 50010.)*

Some Reported Suppresive Organisms (antagonists) of Common Turfgrass Pests

Disease	Antagonist	Reference
Dollar Spot	*Enterobacter cloacae*	Nelson, E.B. and C.M.Craft. 1991. Plant Disease 75: 510-514
Snow Mold	*Typhula phacorrhiza*	Lawton, M.B. and L.L Burpee. 1989. Phytopathology 80:70-73.
Necrotic Ring Spot	*Bacteria, actinomycete*	Melvin, B.P., J.M. Vargas Jr. and W.L. Berndt. 1988. Phytopathology 78:1503-1504.
Brown Patch	*Latersaria arvalis*	Sutker, E.M. and L.T. Lucas. 1987. Phytopathology 77:1721.
Leafy Spurge	*Alternaria angustiovoidea*	Yang, S.M., D.R. Johnson and W.M. Bowler. 1990. Plant Disease 74:601-604.
Japanese beetle grubs	nematodes *(Neoaplectana and Heterorhabditis)*	Shetlar, D.J., P.E. Suleman and R. Georgis. 1988. Journal of Economic Entomology: 81: 1318-1322.

TABLE 3.

7

Population Dynamics

Nature never breaks her own laws.
— Leonardo Da Vinci, inventor and painter

THE TURFGRASS SYSTEM is a complex interaction of plant species, beneficial and harmful organisms and the surrounding environment. This system is comprised of populations, communities and ecosystems. A turfgrass population is a group of plants of the same species occupying a given space or habitat. A habitat is where the organism lives and is characterized by the environmental conditions present. A turfgrass community is the population of all the species, including plants and other organisms living in the same habitat.

And finally the system itself, called a turfgrass ecosystem, is all species living in a habitat and its subsequent interaction with the biotic and abiotic components of the environment. This and the following chapters focus on how turfgrass plants interact with each other, its conditions and resources and the impact of turf managers on these interactions.

The **niche** is the range of abiotic and biotic conditions in which a species can live and reproduce. The niche is often defined by one of two factors (Figure 1) such as temperature and water, which are essential for growth and development. However, an organism's niche is not defined by a few factors, but many factors which have been described as n-dimensional. (Figure 2; Hutchinson, 1957) Multiple-factor combinations are difficult to visualize so discussion of resource affects on plant community dynamics is often limited to three or less.

The niche is further characterized as either **fundamental** or **realized**. The fundamental niche is the entire range of resources and conditions under which an organism can survive. In comparison, the realized niche is the range in which an organism can survive in the face of competition. The realized niche is considerably narrower than the fundamental. (Figure 3) If two competing organisms overlap in their realized niches and enough difference is present, the two species will coexist. If the two competing organisms overlap in their realized niches, but differentiation is not present, one of the organisms will be driven from the habitat. The concept of

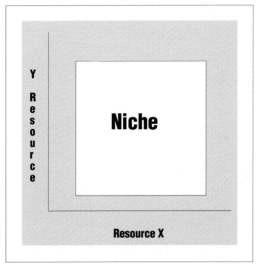

Figure 1. *Within the box defines the limits of growth for an organism. Outside the box the organism cannot survive and reproduce.*

two competing organisms either coexisting or one being driven from the habitat based on their realized niches, is known as the Gause Hypothesis.

An example of one organism driven from the habitat is a turfgrass community composed of Kentucky bluegrass and annual bluegrass. If the mowing height was lowered to a point where Kentucky bluegrass was not competitively adaptive (outside its realized niche) it would not survive in the presence of annual bluegrass.

STABILITY AND COMPLEXITY

Important to turfgrass management is the concept of ecosystem stability and complexity. Stability refers to the community's ability to resist change in the presence of a disturbance. Stability is measured by the speed at which the community returns to its former state. Critical to the ability to resist change is the duration of the disturbance. For example, on a creeping bentgrass putting green the stability of the community is demonstrated when a stress, such as lowering the mowing height below optimum, is imposed. If stress is later alleviated by raising the mowing height and the community has not altered from its prestress state, the community is stable. If the stress resulted in an invasion of competing species such as weeds, the community is considered unstable.

Similar effects occur in high traffic areas. Short durations of traffic on an athletic field may cause damage, but the turf generally returns to its original state. If repeated traffic occurs, however, the turfgrass community will not return to its original composition, but instead develop a considerably different form.

Ecosystem complexity is indicated by the number of turf species. High numbers of species and their associated interactions result in greater stability. The interaction between the turf pathogen *Gaeumannomyces graminis* (take-all patch) and its soil antagonists is an example of complexity leading to stability. (Smith et al, 1989) In a recently fumigated soil, this pathogen is often found to be pervasive causing disruption to the turfgrass community. As time passes and a greater diversity of soil organisms become present, antagonism occurs resulting in a reduction in disease severity. This increase in soil organism diversity results in more

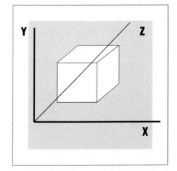

Figure 2. *The conditions and resources that define a niche are too numerous to visualize. In this case, the niche is 3-dimensional.*

stability, and is reflected in fewer disease symptoms. A general rule of thumb regarding turf is: As the system is simplified, the expression of undesirable organisms increases.

Minimal maintenance turf systems characterized by high species diversity and numerous interactions are complex and stable. Devastating pest epidemics in low maintenance situations are unlikely due to the complexity. In intensively maintained turfgrass systems such as a Kentucky bluegrass lawn, plant species diversity and certain specific organisms (pests) are discouraged leading to less complexity. Ironically, as management levels increase and complexity decreases, more management inputs are required to maintain a stable turf system.

Small, incremental increases in complexity do not always lead to an associated increase in stability. For example, seeding mixes containing Kentucky bluegrass and perennial ryegrass are promoted by retailers as a means to enhance stability over a single species. Yet, results from a number of studies comparing mixtures with a monoculture have shown little difference. (Donald, 1963)

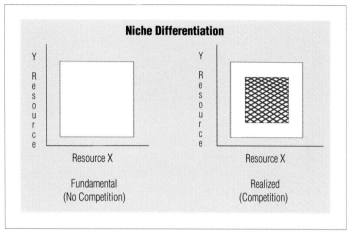

Figure 3. Comparison between the fundamental niche and the realized niche for an organism. The fundamental niche is the region that an organism would occupy without competition. Competition by other organisms restricts the organism to the realized niche (cross-hatched box). See text on pages 93-94.

ENVIRONMENTAL VS. DENSITY-DEPENDENT DYNAMICS

Two approaches to studying population dynamics in turfgrass systems are common. The first approach examines population growth and development as controlled by the environment. This approach is most evident in the development of models for predicting turfgrass disease and insect outbreaks. Some of these models such as the one proposed for predicting anthracnose (Danneberger et al, 1984) are built on statistical methods that show a relationship between certain environmental factors and disease incidence. However, little biological information on the population level or developmental stage of the organism is considered. More consideration of biology is evident in the use of growing degree-days as a means of showing the relationship between organism development and the environment. Degree-day models for insect and plant growth were previously discussed in Chapter 5.

The second approach to population dynamics is the study of density-dependent effects. A population growth rate is governed either directly or indirectly by the resource level and by the presence of predators. Environmental conditions are of less importance in density-dependent interactions. Two major outcomes can occur in density-dependent interactions. In the first, the community and predator population fluctuate but never result in species extinction. In the second, predator populations fluctuate wildly some-

A niche is the abiotic and biotic conditions in which a turfgrass species develop sand grows.

times resulting in species extinction as resources are exhausted. Most of the discussion in this and subsequent chapters revolves around density-dependency.

POPULATION GROWTH

Changes in population size are the result of births and immigration, minus deaths and emigrations. If the number of births for a population are greater than deaths and the trend remains constant, the population will grow at an exponential rate. To sustain exponential growth, unlimited resources and a favorable environment must be present. Fortunately, this is not the case or the Earth would be covered with dandelions, Japanese beetles and humans. For example, if a Kentucky bluegrass turf is susceptible to the pathogen *Drechslera poae* (causal agent of melting-out) and conditions are favorable for disease development, the pathogen will initially begin by infecting a few leaves. As the pathogen develops and reproduces more leaf blades become infected. This cycle of infection and reproduction continues unabated at an exponential rate. Eventually the pathogen numbers will begin to level off. Because of the finite amount of healthy plant tissue available, the pathogen population eventually decreases as the amount of viable tissue available to support the pathogen decreases.

LOGISTIC EQUATION

The most common equation used in ecology to describe population growth is the logistic equation developed by Lotka in the early part of the 20th century. The logistic equation is expressed as:

$$\frac{dN}{dt} = rN \frac{(K - N)}{K}$$

where dN/dt is the growth rate of the population, r is the rate of population increase, N is the population size and K is the carrying capacity of the system. The equation is built on two concepts. First the increase of the population dN/dt (change in N over

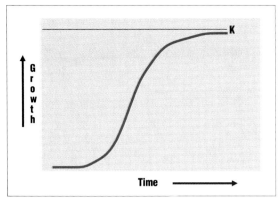

Figure 4. Growth of a population in a niche with limited resources, as predicted by the logistic equation. Carrying capacity (K) represents the maximum number of individuals that can survive in the environment.

time) depends on how big the population (N) is, plus how fast the individual can reproduce (r). The second concept is that the growth rate must decrease as the population approaches the maximum the system can support. Carrying capacity (K) is the term used to describe the maximum number of individuals or plants a given habitat can support. In the logistic equation, (K-N)/K goes to zero as the population (N) approaches the carrying capacity.

Graphically, the logistic equation appears as a S-shaped or sigmoid curve. (Figure 4) It is characterized by an initial slow increase, then a rapid escalation (similar to an exponential growth) followed by a slowing down at the halfway mark. Finally, a flattening of the curve occurs once the limits of growth are reached. Applications of the logistic equation to turfgrass management are most pertinent to pathogen and insects.

N: EFFECT ON PESTS

The initial population size (N) affects how quickly a population can reach its carrying capacity (K). (Figure 5) The larger the initial population, the sooner the population reaches the carrying capacity. In regard to pest management, attempts at reducing the initial population levels of pathogens and destructive insects is an effort to delay the buildup of these pests to plant damaging levels. In some cases, reducing initial N is an economic or environmentally sound approach to pest management.

Reduction in pathogen inoculum and insect populations is accomplished through genetic resistance — destroying

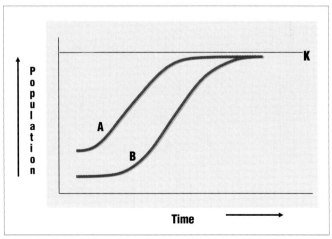

Figure 5. Comparison between two populations with one having a larger initial population (A). The curves are similar except the one with the higher initial population reaches the carrying capacity (K) more rapidly.

97

plant debris that harbor the pests and pesticide applications. A few examples of inoculum reduction are (1) reducing rust through frequent mowing of leaves, thus eliminating spores (ureidiospores) before they mature; (2) reducing the spread of St. Augustine decline virus by cleaning mowing equipment; (3) using powdery mildew resistant cultivars of Kentucky bluegrass in shaded conditions; and (4) diminishing the presence of the adult Kentucky bluegrass billbug or the black turfgrass atenius in the spring with an insecticide application.

In practice, assessing the population levels of pests is difficult; however, insect populations are generally easier to assess than pathogen populations due to the relatively larger size of the insects involved. With most insect pests, population levels are determined by actually counting the individuals or using insect traps. Pathogens on the other hand are microscopic making quantification difficult. Recently, disease test kits have been developed to provide a qualitative assessment of pathogen levels. (Miller et al, 1990)

In devising management strategies targeted at population levels, consideration of the population's growth rate is important. If the relative growth rate of a pathogen is high, reduction of initial inoculum has minimal effect. For example, Pythium propagules in soil and thatch are the source for blight epidemics. (Hall, et al, 1980) Although reduction of thatch may be a logical means of reducing the Pythium blight incidence, this is probably not efficient given Pythium can develop explosively from even a very tiny population. However, if the rate of pest increase is slow, reducing inoculum or pest levels will be more effective.

r: RATE OF GROWTH

Rate of reproduction greatly influences population levels. (Figure 6) If reproduction or "births" is equal to mortality, no population growth occurs. If reproduction is greater than mortality then the population will increase. Rate with regard to pest problems is governed by the reproductive potential (generation time), the availability and susceptibility of the host and the environmental effects of the interaction.

Cultural practices designed to minimize pest problems may reduce the growth rate. Any cultural practice that creates environmental conditions unfavorable for reproduction and growth will reduce r. Examples of cultural practices that reduce r include: (1) increasing air movement through

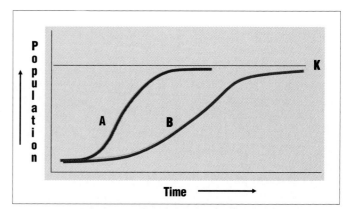

Figure 6. Comparison between two populations developing according to the logistic equation but with different rates (r). Population growth is more rapid with a higher r value (A).

removal of brush around a green, or improving drainage to reduce the conditions favorable for pythium blight; (2) irrigating a turf to promote *Beauveria* spp. which is a natural fungal disease of chinchbugs; and (3) applying adequate amounts of nitrogen to reduce the growth rate of *Colletotrichum graminicula,* the causal agent of anthracnose. (Danneberger et al, 1983) Additional examples of cultural practices affecting population size or rate are provided in Table 1. As previously mentioned, reducing N and r slows pest population growth to damaging levels. The longer the period needed for pest development, the greater likelihood environmental conditions will become less favorable.

In turfgrass seed production, one method of reducing the pest population is to burn the fields.

K: CARRYING CAPACITY
The carrying capacity is the maximum population size that can be supported by a given habitat. (Figure 4) Turfgrass managers have the capability of raising or lowering the carrying capacity of the system through managed inputs. For example, well-fertilized and watered turf can support more plants and potentially more pests such as white grubs or bluegrass billbugs than a turf receiving minimal fertilization. Under natural conditions limits to growth such as temperature, competition for limited resources and predators frequently restrict a population's ability to reach the carrying capacity. In turf, however, management practices allow growth to be maintained close to the carrying capacity or increase it through nutritional programs and pest control.

DISRUPTIONS IN STABLE GROWTH: OSCILLATIONS
In any system growth limits are imposed by factors such as space, nutrients and energy availability. The increased competition between individuals for these factors may result in mortality. Changes in climate, genetic makeup, predators and human intervention all promote fluctuations in populations. In low maintenance situations, plant growth is relatively stable with little population fluctuation. The potential for severe population oscillations is greatest in monoculture systems with high energy inputs. If these oscillations become severe, chaos can occur resulting in the "crashing" of the plant community. (Figure 7)

In a recent study, high nitrogen soil levels led to chaotic behavior in a perennial grass system which researchers attributed to increased plant litter due to high nitrogen levels. (Tilman and Wedlin 1991). In turf, the combination of nitrogen rate and carrier may also induce wide oscillations in plant growth. Quick-release nitrogen sources have the potential to cause rapid plant growth in a very short period of time with a subsequent decrease in plant growth after the nitrogen is used up. Cyclic fluctuations in plant growth with repeated high application rates of quick-release nitrogen may eventually lead to detrimental turfgrass effects. Slow-release sources provide a more moderate growth rate and can result in less growth fluctuation and fewer chances of the system crashing.

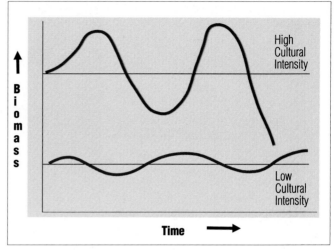

Figure 7. The dark linear line represents a baseline for stable growth. Actual growth is oscillating with greater amplitudes occurring at high cultural intensity levels which, if great enough, can result in chaos.

In turf, "plant litter" often takes the form of thatch which is detrimental to plant growth. Subsequently, its control or management is critical to successfully maintaining a healthy turf. As such, it is interesting to speculate about the importance of plant litter recycling in turfgrass ecosystems and provide insight into the stability of a system. In forests or grasslands, the detritus is a very important portion of energy recycling. The decomposing insects, fungi and other soil organisms living off dead material, rather than the surface green tissue, provide stability to the system. High energy input turf systems such as putting greens or athletic fields on modified systems may actually lack the variety of decomposing organisms that brings some stability to the system.

In a perennial turfgrass system the likelihood of severe oscillations or chaos developing is probably rare. Wide fluctuations in the growth of a turfgrass species resulting in a "crash" (death) would likely result in its displacement by some other species. However, further work on chaotic behavior is needed in turf to discover what, if any effects, cultural practices have.

In summary, the difficulty in maintaining a high input system may not be from the increased complexity of the system but actually from a lack of complexity. Thus, management practices such as lowering the mowing height, improper irrigation and fertilization and improper chemical use may actually increase the potential for major fluctuations in community growth.

Cultural Practices that Can Reduce Inoculum Levels or Impact Growth Rate

Disease	Cultural Practices
Anthracnose	Moderate levels of nitrogen (0.5 lbs./1,000 sq. ft.) applied monthly during the summer stress time lowers the level of infection and disease severity. Minimize the time free moisture is on the leaf blade. The longer leaf exudates or free moisture is present, the greater chance infection will take place.
Copper Spot	Increasing nitrogen level helps discourage disease. Liming may also be a beneficial practice to minimize the disease severity.
Dollar Spot	Adequate to high levels of nitrogen will discourage dollar spot formation. Remove any excess moisture whether it be leaf exudates or water. Encourage air movement especially around putting greens to reduce humidity levels. This may entail thinning or removing trees or undergrowth. Irrigate judiciously during periods of dollar spot activity. Avoid droughty soils.
Red Thread	Maintain adequate fertility levels especially nitrogen. Irrigate during drought conditions since this disease is most severe on slow growing turfs.
Powdery Mildew	If planting Kentucky bluegrass in a shaded situation, use powdery mildew resistant cultivars. Provide adequate fertilization and water to encourage growth. Provide as much sunlight to the turf as possible.
Yellow Tuft	Provide adequate drainage to turfgrass sites most likely to be infected by this pathogen. Disease symptoms can be reduced with nitrogen applications that promote growth. However, nitrogen will not cure the disease.
The Smuts	There are no satisfactory cultural controls for this disease. In non-irrigated situations the plants will die in the summer but the disease tends not to spread. However, in irrigated situations the disease becomes more severe. The best cultural practice is to plant resistant cultivars.
Rust	Adequate watering and fertilization should be provided to sustain growth and allow the plant to survive additional stresses that may occur.
Leaf Spot	Avoid excessive application of nitrogen in the spring. Judicious applications are recommended. Avoid the use of certain fungicides and herbicides. Some of these products actually encourage formation. For example, sterol inhibiting fungicides applied to creeping bentgrass in the spring appears to enhance disease development.

TABLE 1.

Snow Mold	Avoid heavy applications of nitrogen six weeks prior to the turfgrass going dormant. Lush growth encourages this disease. Mow the grass until it goes dormant. Allowing the turf to grow above the mowing height results in greater disease damage. To promote recovery in the spring, encourage active growth.
Brown Patch	Attempts should be made to minimize moisture levels by good subsurface and surface drainage, provide adequate air circulation and remove any dew or moisture from the turf. These practices help reduce the humidity levels around the turfgrass plant. Avoid excessive nitrogen applications during periods conducive for brown patch.
Pythium Blight	Avoid places where excessive water can accumulate. Provide good drainage from low lying areas and on clayey soils. In areas where air movement is poor, trim trees to encourage drier conditions. Research has found that a large population of spores accumulate in thatch. Thatch reduction and control should be practiced in areas where Pythium is likely to occur.
Southern Blight	No cultural practices currently are known for controlling or minimizing Southern blight.
Spring Dead Spot	Minimizing nitrogen applications to bermudagrass in the spring is helpful. Recent work has identified the use of acidifying fertilizers (i.e., ammonium-based) as reducing disease incidence (Dernoeden et al, 1991).
Take-All Patch	This disease is difficult to control and little if any chemical control can be achieved. The use of ammonium chloride as a nitrogen source appears to reduce the disease severity.
Necrotic Ring Spot	Not a lot of information is available on recently identified patch diseases such as necrotic ring spot, summer patch and take-all patch. However, light frequent irrigation appears to minimize this disease. Nitrogen applications will help promote recovery. Promote good root growth by core aeration. Avoid prolonged water-saturated turf.
Bermudagrass Decline	All bermudagrass cultivars to date are susceptible. Fertilize adequately with nitrogen and potassium and use acidifying fertilizers.

TABLE 1.   *(Compiled from Smith et al, 1989; Smiley et al, 1992; and Vargas, 1981).*

8

Intraspecific Competition

For the biologist there are no classes — only individuals.
Jean Rostand, French scientist

INTRASPECIFIC COMPETITION is the interaction between individuals of the same species brought about by shared requirements for a limited resource. Competition can occur among individuals of grasses, weeds, pathogen strains and insect strains. Intraspecific competition in grasses may be detrimental to plants because of a decreased rate of resource uptake per plant, decreased growth and an increased susceptibility to pests.

Competitive effects are measured predominantly through weight accumulation and tillering capabilities. Biomass which is the weight of the living material is often expressed in ecological studies as the weight per individual. In turf, the number of individuals is so great that *population* biomass for a given area is used. In the context of this chapter, biomass is the weight of the aboveground living plant material (usually removed through mowing) per given area (square foot, square meter, etc.). For density, individual plants are normally used in most ecological studies. In turf, however, individual plants are not usually recognizable so tillers are treated as the basic unit. (Lush and Franz, 1991) In this text, density is expressed as tillers per given area.

Plants do not directly interact with each other, but compete indirectly through close association. A plant can gain an advantage over a neighboring plant by "tapping" a resource sooner or with greater efficiency than another causing a "resource depletion zone." Resource depletion zones refer to the absence or reduced levels of light, water and nutrients within an area. The indirect interaction of plants in close association is termed exploitation. (Bergon et al, 1990) The intensity of this competition is dependent on the amount of the resource available and on the plant density. Competition is greater as the number of plants per area are increased. Intraspecific competition compared to interspecific (between different species) is more intensive because individuals of the same species share the same niche.

Intraspecific competition in turfgrasses develops progressively from establishment to maturity. In a newly seeded turf very little competition occurs among seedlings. Any mortality that does occur reflects chance, parental effects (genetics) or defoliation/damage brought about by pest organisms. As the seedlings develop and grow, mortality increases as the individual tillers begin to compete for resources. Plants continue to grow, albiet more slowly than they would if they were widely spaced. At this point, growth is no longer independent of density. Eventually, as tiller density increases so does competition until a point is reached where some plants continue to grow only if others die.

TURFGRASS ESTABLISHMENT: SEED PREPARATION

A close look at seedling turf reveals a number of factors influencing competition. These factors include the genetic and physiological state of the seed as well as the seedling density. Plant species, cultivars and seed lot variations will cause differences in germination rates and seedling vigor. The result is differential growth among the seeds, with the "survival of the fittest" being the rule. For example, blending is the process of combining two or more cultivars of the same species at the same site for more genetic diversity. Blending also has the potential to provide better adaptation. However, if a quickly germinating cultivar shades the slower germinating cultivar, a disproportionate level of the quick germinating cultivar might occur. A low seed vigor lot would suffer the same fate as a slow germinating lot. The result may be a shift in the turf composition.

Seeds modified through a symbiotic relationship between the seed and an organism, preconditioning or seed coating may have an advantage over non-modified seed. Symbiotic relationships between an individual species member and a fungus may provide an advantage in establishment over a non-symbiotic individual. Tall fescue and some cultivars of perennial ryegrass are infected with a fungal endophyte *(Acremonium coenophiallum)*. (Table 1) Seeds from endophyte-infected plants have a higher rate of germination and produce more biomass and tillers than seeds from uninfected plants. (Clay, 1987; Rice et al, 1990) Additionally, endophyte-containing tall fescue and perennial ryegrass cultivars are more resistant to surface-feeding insects.

Preconditioning seeds by pregermination or osmoconditioning, is an attempt to enhance germination and establishment of turfgrasses in the presence of suboptimal environmental conditions. Pregermination involves partially germinating seeds before they are sown for the purpose of shortening the germination period. (Dudeck and Peacock, 1986) Disadvantages to pregermination include the need for immediate planting after treatment and difficulties with uniform seed dispersion because of high seed moisture content. Osmoconditioning is a seed treatment that preconditions seeds in an osmoticum and allows the seed some water uptake. Osmoconditioning has an advantage in that after treatment, the seeds can be dried and safely stored. During osmoconditioning, the seed's biochemical processes are initiated, but the seed is not allowed to germinate. Thus, the seed may be air dried and stored like non-treated seed since germination does not occur during osmoconditioning. Osmoconditioning appears to be more effective on slowly germinating seeds such as Kentucky bluegrass, and not as effective on rapidly germinating seeds such as perennial ryegrass. (Danneberger et al, 1992; Lush and Birkhead, 1987)

Seed coating is an attempt to add necessary nutrients to the seed to enhance germination or a chemical protectant for safeguard against potential pests upon germination. Fertilizer and lime coatings have enhanced seed germination and may provide an alternative to soil incorporation of fertilizer and lime where proper seedbed preparation is not feasible. (Hathcock, et al, 1984) In situations where seedling diseases occur, seeds treated with a fungicide may provide a competitive advantage over non-treated seeds.

Once seeds have emerged and developed a full turf canopy, the introduction of new individuals through overseeding is difficult due to the exclusion of light and existing competition for below ground resources. In turf renovation, the turf must be thinned and the soil exposed to have a successful seeding establishment. By thinning the existing stand, light becomes available to new seedlings and if the seeds are placed in contact with unoccupied soil, nutrients and water are available for uptake.

SELF-THINNING

As previously mentioned, competition can reach a point in a turfgrass stand where growth can only occur at the death of others. When plants die, making space available for the development of others, the process of self-thinning is occurring. Earlier in this chapter, portions of the self-thinning principle were briefly mentioned. The self-thinning principle is described here in more detail.

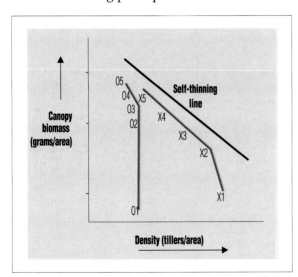

Figure 1. Comparison of growth and development of grass species as influenced by seeding density (O = low seeding, X = high seeding density). This graph is based on data of Lonsdale and Watkinson, 1982. (See text for further explanation.)

The self-thinning process can be explained by comparing two newly seeded turfs of the same species — one seeded at a relatively low density and the other at a higher density. (Figure 1) In this figure, the less dense turf is designated as O while the higher density turf is designated X. The numerical designation next to either the O or X refers to the same point in time. For example, O2 and X2 refer to the population biomass and density of each stand at the same instance. At the first sampling date (O1 vs. X1), the emerging seedlings are roughly the same size. However, since the low density seedling turf has fewer individuals it also has a lower biomass. As both seedling populations grow, competition begins to occur between the individuals. The competition occurs sooner in the denser stand (the number of tillers decreases at X2 vs. X1). In addition, the growth rate of the plants at the higher density is greatly slowed (biomass of X2 vs. O2). At some point, the two populations reach a point of full canopy cover (O3 and X2).

At the lower density seeded stand the plants are fewer, but larger as reflected in the amount of biomass. At the denser seeded stand, a greater number of individuals are present but are less dense. Full canopy cover may be thought of as the carrying capacity of the turfgrass stand, as well as represent the starting point where self-thinning begins to occur (self-thinning line). Carrying capacity, as discussed in Chapter 7, is the number of individuals that can be supported by a habitat. A variety of organism populations have the potential to overshoot the carrying capacity. However, increased mortality beyond the carrying capacity of the habitat will eventually bring the population down below the given capacity. Traditionally, plants do not overshoot the carrying capacity (self-thinning line). Ballare and colleagues (1990, 1992) have shown that neighboring plants "sense" each other's presence via phytochrome by picking up radiation reflected (far-red) by nearby leaves and changing their growth characteristics (i.e., reduced tillering) well before their resources are reduced.

Once the populations reach the self-thinning line, further population growth is subject to severe competition resulting in some plant death. The loss of individual plants is more than compensated for by growth through the surviving plants (X5 > X4 > X3>X2 and O5 > O4 > O3). The relationship between biomass is now the opposite of the initial plant population; the least dense population has the highest biomass. (Lush, 1990)

Practical examples of this self-thinning principle as applied to sowing density include the establishment of a new putting green and a sod field. A superintendent may contemplate sowing at a high rate to get a quicker cover on the putting green. However, at the higher sowing rate, mortality will occur once full canopy cover is achieved and the plant population moves up the self-thinning line. Over time,

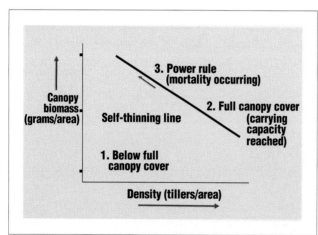

Figure 2. The diagonal line indicates the theoretical carrying capacity of the turf. Plants located along the upper left hand area of the diagonal are fewer, larger, more developed and coarser than those located at the lower right hand end. Two major regions are 1) the area below which full cover is not achieved and little competition between plants exists and 2) the line itself where full cover is achieved and competition between individuals is occurring.

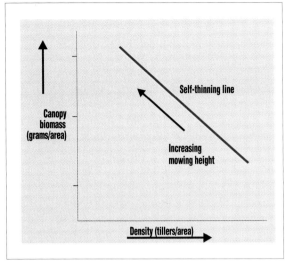

Figure 3. Increasing mowing height increases biomass at the expense of density.

[Figure labels: Canopy biomass (grams/area); Self-thinning line; Increasing mowing height; Density (tillers/area)]

the turf sowed at a high density will become comparable to the turf sowed at the lower density. In this case there is no long-term benefit to using a high seeding rate.

Sod growers often sow at or below the recommended sowing rate to enhance individual plant development which is reflected in greater rhizome or stolon growth. By enhancing rhizome and/or stolon growth the sod is more intertwined, will be harvested sooner and will not fall apart. At a high sowing rate, plants are hindered in their development (the price of achieving full canopy cover quickly). As such, the sod can not be harvested as quickly at a lower sowing density.

Alternatively, the use of high sowing rates to delay plant growth and development is the rationale behind overseeding warm-season turfs, specifically putting greens. High initial density provides a quick turf cover, and the lack of growth and development causes the plants to remain in a juvenile stage. Consequently, a lower height of cut is achieved since juvenile plants are able to tolerate lower heights of cut than can be expected from a mature plant of the same species.

In summary, should turf density exist below the self-thinning line (Figure 2, point 1), full canopy cover is not achieved and little competition between the plants occurs. As the stand matures and full canopy cover is achieved (Figure 2, point 2), the competition increases. Once the self-thinning line is reached, further growth results in severe competition with changes occurring in population density and biomass. (Figure 2, point 3) At this stage, the least dense population has the highest biomass and the populations conform to what is known as the power rule.

The actual slope of the self-thinning line for turfgrasses is -1/2, (Lush, 1990) and is calculated by dividing the bio-

Recommended or slightly lower seeding rates are used by sod growers to promote growth and development (more rhizomes, stolons and roots) vs. a high seeding rate which provides quick cover but little plant development. A lower seeding rate sod vs. a higher seeding rate sod is harvested sooner. (Photo: Courtesy of Mike Fast)

mass by the tiller numbers. (See Lush 1990 for more detailed discussion.) The numerical value of the slope of the self-thinning line has recently undergone increased scrutiny. In population systems like forests, biomass is calculated on an individual (i.e., one tree) basis instead of the total biomass per given area as used in turf. The self-thinning lines based on weight per individual has a slope of -3/2. In the early 1980s the -3/2 slope was described as one of the more widespread principles in plant population ecology. (White, 1980) Recently, the validity of -3/2 slope has undergone criticism to the point where it does not seem to hold true in all situations. (Lonsdale, 1990) However, the self-thinning principle with a line slope of -1/2 does hold true for turfgrasses. (Lush, 1992)

CULTURAL PRACTICES AND EFFECTS ON THE DYNAMICS OF SELF-THINNING
Mary Lush (1990) has looked at the impact of cultural practices on turfgrass populations in relation to the self-thinning principle. Below are some applications of her work with an emphasis on the generalization of community dynamics.

Plant characteristics along the self-thinning line. Plants located on the upper left hand area of the self-thinning line are bigger but fewer in number than plants located on the lower right hand part of the line. (Figure 2) Plants along the left hand portion of the line are: Able to tolerate wear because bigger and more developed plants are more tolerant than smaller plants; coarser in texture; and possibly less prone to disease since a low density turf in some instances is less susceptible than a high density turf. Table 2 provides some examples of turfgrasses and their location along the self-thinning line.

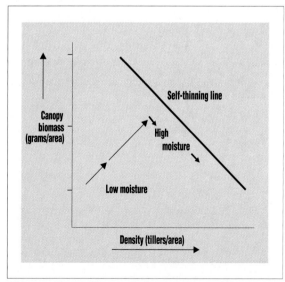

Figure 4. *Increasing moisture increases plant density and biomass until the self-thinning line is reached. At this point, increasing moisture increases density at the expense of biomass.*

Mowing height is considered one of if not the most significant cultural practice. Mowing height influences community makeup and the amount of resources needed for maintenance. Additionally, mowing height affects the biomass and density of a turf. At high cutting heights, the stand's plant density decreases and the biomass increases. (Figure 3) From a management perspective, larger plants are more tolerant to wear.

Moisture influences the biomass and density of a turf. (Figure 4) If moisture is limited and turf growth is occurring below the self-thinning line, the addition of water will increase both the biomass and density. If the

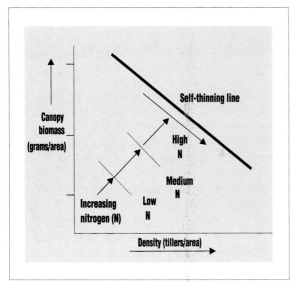

Figure 5. Increased nitrogen input will increase biomass and density of a turf until the carrying capacity line is reached. At this point, increasing nitrogen expands plant density with simultaneous decrease in individual plant size. Low, medium and high refer to relative levels of nitrogen applications.

turf community is at a point along the self-thinning line, the addition of excessive water will increase density at the expense of biomass. In situations where wear tolerance is a concern, such as athletic fields, the addition of water to a droughty field will increase plant development and ultimately increase wear tolerance. However, if the field is at capacity the addition of water will result in decreased plant size and a decrease in wear tolerance.

Nitrogen applied to the turf can raise the carrying capacity of a turf community. In Figure 5, the application of nitrogen can move the self-thinning line upward thus supporting more plants at greater weights. For example at a low nitrogen level, an increase in nitrogen to a medium level will result in a positive increase in density and biomass. An additional positive increment can be achieved with a higher rate of nitrogen. However, at this point, nitrogen is no longer a limiting factor for growth and additional increments will not raise the self-thinning line. What occurs is a movement down the self thinning line in response to more nitrogen. The result is an increase in plant density at the expense of individual plant biomass. The net effect on the community is decreased wear tolerance and the possibility of increased disease incidence. Identifying the capacity of the system is difficult. As a result, incremental additions of nitrogen beyond the optimum are not visually observable until wear is introduced. (Canaway and Hacker, 1988)

Interaction of mowing and ni-

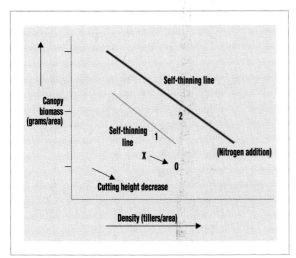

Figure 6. Interaction of mowing and fertilization. (See text for explanation.)

trogen on density and biomass. Previously, individual factor effects on density and plant size were discussed without considering possible interactions. The association between nitrogen fertilization and mowing heights on putting greens is routinely faced by golf course superintendents. If mowing is viewed as a baseline together with moderate levels of nitrogen, the turf is at full cover as seen at point 1 in Figure 6. With the addition of nitrogen we can raise the level of density and biomass to point 2. Turf managers facing the challenge of providing fast greens are currently trying to minimize growth through eliminating or greatly reducing nitrogen applications. The effect is a reduction in plant numbers and biomass. (X in Figure 6) Less dense, smaller plants may result in faster greens by reducing resistance to ball roll, but at the cost of full cover. To increase the density of turf, a lawn care operator or golf course superintendent needs to lower the height of cut to increase shoot numbers. Even so, full cover will still not be achieved. The result is undesirable weeds filling void areas. In this situation, nitrogen has become a limiting factor for growth.

INTRASPECIFIC COMPETITION IN PEST POPULATIONS

Intraspecific competition, to date, has dealt with turfgrass plants. However, intraspecific competition may occur in many different species. In natural systems, host density influences pest infection rates or pest populations. A high host density favors infection and growth of the pest (pathogen or insect) population. The result is a decline in the host population, followed by a decline in the pest population. (Figure 7) The oscillation in host density mimicked by the pest population is described as being in dynamic equilibrium. (Burdon and Chilvers, 1982)

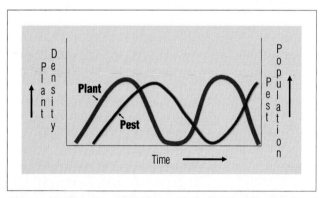

Figure 7. The relationship between plant populations (density) and pest populations. Pest populations mimic plant populations. As the amount of tissue available for pest attack increases so does the pest population. When the amount of healthy plant tissue decreases, so does the pest population.

Pesticides have been used to reduce plant fluctuations due to pests. The introduction of synthetic chemicals for controlling insects, diseases and weeds, however, has in some instances resulted in chemically resistant pest populations. Resistance to insecticides, fungicides and herbicides has occurred in many plant systems, including turfgrasses. (Table 3) Turf managers should be most concerned with disease resistance when numerous fungicide applications are used. Insect and weed resistance is of minor concern on turf because of the fewer number of insecticide and herbicide applications made during a year. A notable exception is the application of insecticides in the Southern United States for chinchbug control.

This shift from chemically sensitive to chemically resistant populations brought about by the changes in allele frequency (genetics of resistance) are discussed below. Pesticide resistance occurs when resistant alleles predominate over sensitive alleles in the pest population. The understanding and development of strategies to avoid or minimize pesticide resistance is critical to successfully maintaining high quality turf and golf courses.

FUNGICIDE RESISTANCE

Turf systems with high density and uniform species composition are routinely afflicted by diseases which reduce the density of the turf. Unlike natural systems, where quality is not a concern, turf managers must maintain a uniform turf for aesthetic and functional purposes. Although, cultural practices help to reduce disease severity, fungicide applications are sometimes needed in a successful management program.

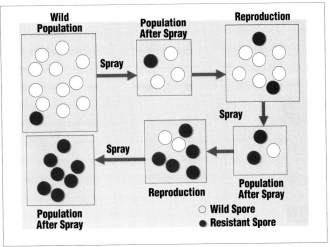

Fungi have sexual and asexual reproduction cycles. Sexual reproduction provides fungi the opportunity to mix genes

Figure 8. Buildup of a resistant spore population through the repeated application of a site-specific fungicide.

from two individuals to get new and unique individuals. Another method for developing individuals with new gene combinations is anastomosis — asexual reproduction — which is the union of hypha resulting in an intermixing of contents. The more common form of reproduction for most turfgrass pathogens is asexual.

A pest population with a natural sensitivity to a fungicide is known as a "wild type." In such a situation, a small number of individuals with resistance to a pesticide may exist within a population even though that chemical has never been applied. Resistance becomes a major concern to the turf manager when the wild types are selectively removed through pesticide applications and the resistant types flourish and cause damage. (Figure 8) Dekker (1976) has proposed five mechanisms by which resistant individuals avoid the toxic effects of pesticides:

* **Decreased permeability.** The resistant type does not absorb as much of the pesticide as the wild types.
* **Metabolism.** The resistant type detoxifies the pesticide or reduces the release of the compound.

111

* **Decreased affinity at the site of action.** Some fungicides are known to attack specific sites in a pathogen. A modification in the resistant fungus site of action can make the fungicide ineffective. For example, the fungicide benomyl binds to a protein subunit of the spindle microtubules in growing fungi, resulting in inhibition of mitosis and eventual death. A slight change in the protein subunit found in resistant strains of the fungus prevents binding by benomyl.
* **Circumvention of the site of action.** Circumvention means that the pest has an alternative metabolic pathway for the one blocked by the pesticide.
* **Compensation.** A resistant pathogen has the ability to increase the production of an inhibited substance. For example, if a fungicide inhibits a certain enzyme, the resistant pathogen has the ability to increase the production of that enzyme.

Minimizing the risk of fungicide resistance depends on selecting fungicides based on its specific mode of action and resistance potential. Subsequently, the mode of action of these products has great significance in the understanding and managing of resistance.

Fungicides that are surface protectants (kill fungi outside the plant) with minimal systemic activity such as chlorothalonil, anilazine, PCNB and dithiocarbamates, have lower risk of resistance with continual applications because they affect many metabolic processes of the fungi (multisite activity). The sterol inhibiting fungicides (i.e., triademifon, fenarimol, propiconazole) have a greater potential for developing resistance than the protectants, but not as great as the benzimidazoles. Although the sterol inhibitors are site-specific, they are considered to have low to moderate resistant risks. (Dekker, 1985) Resistance to sterol inhibitors has been observed on non-turf crops (Koller and Scheinpflug, 1987) but only recently on turf. (Vargas, 1992) Dicarboximide fungicides (iprodione, vinclozolin) pose a moderate potential for resistance problems. Fungicides posing a high likelihood of resistance are the compounds classified as the benzimidazoles (benomyl, thiophanate-methyl) and phenylamides (metalaxyl).

Three strategies exist for using fungicides, each with different potential for resistance. The first strategy is the continuous use of a fungicide. If the fungicide is site-specific (as all are except for the protectants), the likelihood of resistance is great. The second strategy is alternating. Alternating fungicides of different modes of action is a common practice to delay resistance. Alternating fungicides with similar modes of action such as benomyl and thiophanate-methyl has no advantage because a fungus resistant to one is also resistant to the other (multiple resistance). An additional concern with alternating is that a fungus may develop resistance against two or more fungicides with different modes of action, such as has been detected with benomyl and iprodione on dollar spot. (Detweiler et al, 1983)

The third strategy is mixing which is combining fungicides from different classes in one mix. Mixtures are combinations of fungicides from different classes applied simultaneously. Advantages to mixtures include the following: Control is not left to one mode of action, the chances of resistance are less if total pathogen population levels are kept low and it is a possible synergistic effect for disease control. The major

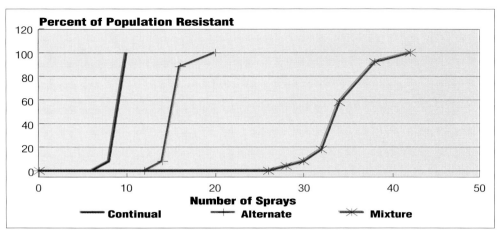

Figure 9. Resistant population buildup with different fungicide application strategies. This simulation assumes 90 percent efficacy and equal fitness between wild and resistant spores.

disadvantages to mixtures are: Matching days of control for two or more fungicides, possible antagonistic effects between fungicides and the expense.

In attempting to reduce the cost of mixing fungicides, Sanders (1985) has shown that metalaxyl resistance can be delayed by mixing half rates of metalaxyl with another pythium controlling fungicide. Excellent control of Pythium blight can still be achieved. Sanders (1985) has also found excellent dollar spot suppression with half rate, two-component mixtures of benzimidazoles, dicarboximides and sterol inhibitors. Additionally, Couch and Smith (1991) found the synergistic effects with fractional rates of pythium controlling fungicides. In their study, a mixture of fungicides at fractional rates provided better control than each fungicide alone at the full rate. In some instances, however, Couch and Smith (1991) reported antagonistic effects with certain fungicide mixes.*

The effectiveness of continual, alternating and mixing of fungicides in an attempt to reduce the likelihood of disease can be demonstrated graphically using a computer simulation model based on work by Flemming (1981), Kable and Jeffery (1980). A key component in the development of a resistant fungus population is the population's "fitness." Fitness is a general term used to describe how adapted the fungus population is in the environment once it predominates. In the first simulation the fitness of the resistant type was the same as the wild type. Resistance occurred for all combinations except in the number of sprays needed before resistance dominated the population. This number decreased in the following order: mixtures > alternating > straight (continual). (Figure 9) In the second simulation, the fitness of the resistant type is reduced in half compared to the wild type. Fungicide resistance occurs at a slower rate than the first simulation for continual and alternating sprays, but resistance is not detected in the mixture. (Figure 10)

Once resistance develops an important question is, "Will resistance persist?" In

*Always follow manufacturers recommended label rates and combinations.

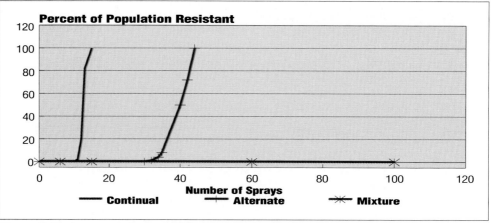

Figure 10. Resistant population buildup as influenced by spray program. In this simulation the resistant spores are assumed to be half as fit as the wild types. Efficacy of the fungicide is 90 percent.

practical terms, this is simply asking whether a particular fungicide can ever be used successfully once the resistant fungi predominate. The answer depends on the fitness of the fungus. Benomyl resistant types have fitness similar or greater than the wild types. Once resistance has occurred to benomyl the population remains resistant for a long time even in the absence of the fungicide. (Sanders et al, 1982; Sanders, 1983) On the other hand, resistance to iprodione appears to have a lesser fitness. In the absence of a fungicide, the wild type predominates and resistant strains drop to a lower level. (Detweiler et al, 1983)

Skylakakis (1983) concluded that resistance could be minimized by any means that will slow disease development such as changes in the weather, cultural practices or host resistance; as well as the decrease in the fitness of the resistant population as the risk of resistance also decreases. To reduce the chance of fungicide resistance, disease resistant cultivars, cultural practices and, where applicable, biological controls need to be effectively used to minimize the number of fungicide treatments.

INSECTICIDE RESISTANCE

Considerable work has been done to determine the causes of insecticide resistance as many insects are able to tolerate most synthetic pesticides. In an extreme case, the Colorado potato beetle on Long Island, N.Y., developed resistance to all major classes of insecticides. (Forgash, 1984)

In numerous studies, it has been shown that insecticide resistance is controlled by a single gene in the insect. Insects are diploid, meaning they carry two copies of each chromosome which in turn has numerous genes. Each gene has two

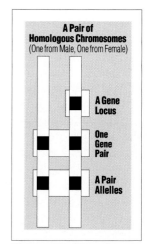

Figure 11. Homologous chromosomes.

copies. The two chromosomes carrying the gene are referred to as homologous chromosomes. The location of a gene on the chromosome is called a locus. (Figure11) The genes for a protein may be somewhat different. For example, one gene may confer resistance while the other may be a wild type. These various forms of a gene are called alleles.

If both alleles are the same they are termed homozygous. An example is if the alleles (corresponding genes on both chromosomes) both conferred susceptibility to a particular insecticide (SS; S= susceptibility). Heterozygous, on the other hand, creates a situation in which two different alleles are paired in an insect such as the combination of genes for susceptibility and resistance (SR; S = susceptibility, R = resistance). Finally, if one allele such as susceptibility is dominant — (S) vs. a recessive resistant (r) — the combination is (Sr) but the expression of this trait is susceptible. That is, only the susceptible gene is expressed.

Looking at the genetic makeup of resistance, three types of gene combinations can be determined: the homozygous susceptible (SS), resistant (RR) and the heterozygote (SR) that carry both susceptible and resistant genes. In a natural system, a homozygous resistant (RR) population is small. (Figure 12) If the resistant allele is dominant (i.e., expressed even in the SR combination), individuals with the gene may have a tremendous advan-

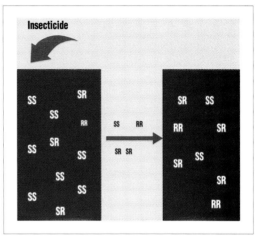

Figure 12. Insecticide effects on insect population. (See text for explanation.)

tage when the pesticide of concern is used. This was the case with dieldrin resistance, which is dominant, expressing itself in the population quickly. However, if the resistant gene is recessive, expression of the resistant population takes considerably longer. This occurred with diazinon resistance. (McKenzie and Whitten, 1984)

Insecticide resistance is dependent on the frequency, number and dominance of the resistance alleles. The likelihood of a resistant insect population developing quickly is greater if the initial resistant population is high. This is hard to determine since variability exists in any insect population. The dominance of the resistant gene is important in the expression of insect resistance. A recessive insecticide resistant gene will take longer to express itself in the population vs. a dominant resistant gene. From a management perspective, the use of insecticides should be similar to that of fungicides.

Some Turfgrass Varieties Containing Acremonium Endophytes

Variety	% Infection	Variety	% Infection
		Perennial Ryegrass	
Yorktown III	97	Palmer II	97
Gen-90	97	Express	97
Advent	97	APM	97
Seville	96	Dandy	96
Duet	93	Manhattan II	93
Prelude II	93	Repell II	92
Assure	92	Pleasure	92
Target	92	Riviera	91
Gettysburg	91	Pennant	91
Legacy	90	4 Del. Dwarf	90
Pinnacle	90	Repell	89
SR 4200	89	Commander	88
Regal	86	Saturn	85
Competitor	71	Accolade	70
Equal	68	Calypso	66
Citation	59	Stallion	58
Callente	54	Premier	50
Entrar	47	Prestige	43
Derby Supreme	38	Lindsay	37
Charger	34	Envy	30
		Tall Fescue	
Titan	98	Shenandoah	86
Mesa	70	Tribute	58
Aguara	50	Arid	48
Normarc 99	42	Rebel Jr.	37
Trident	28	Rebel II	28
		Fine Fescue	
Jamestown II	100	Reliant	100
Warwick	96	Southport	94
SR 5000	92	SR 3000	64
Rainbow	63	Valda	47

TABLE 1.

Relationships Between Biomass and Density for Selected Turfgrass Species

	Comment
Turfgrass species (in general)	Turfgrasses such as Kentucky bluegrass, perennial ryegrass and tall fescue are most suited to higher densities with small plant size. Finer texture species, such as creeping bentgrass, are most suited to higher densities with small plant size.
Perennial ryegrass	In athletic fields, a larger plant is more resistant to wear than a smaller, denser turf. A higher height of cut will promote greater plant development resulting in increased wear tolerance.
Creeping bentgrass	This grass type is usually mowed short to increase density for such things as providing a means for a golf ball to "sit up." On putting greens, a shorter turf may be more dense, but the wear tolerance will be reduced. Thus, if a golf course has minimal play the turf can generally mowed shorter with limited loss of quality. However, on a golf course with considerable play, the lower height will make the bentgrass less tolerant to wear.

TABLE 2.

Reported Cases of Fungicide Resistance Occurring in Turfgrass Situations

FUNGICIDES

Fungus	Disease	Reported	Host	Fungicide(Reference)
Sclerotinia homoeocarpa	dollar spot	1968	bentgrass	cadmium succinate[2]
Erysiphe graminus	powdery mildew	1973	bluegrass	benomyl[6]
S. homoeocarpa	dollar spot	1974	putting green	benomyl[8]
Fusarium nivale	pink snow mold	1982	*bent/poa*	iprodione[1]
S. homoeocarpa	dollar spot	1983	bentgrass	iprodione[3]
Pythium aphanidermatum	pythium blight	1984	bentgrass	metalaxyl[4]
Colletotrizchun graminicola	anthracnose	1989	bentgrass	benomyl[5]
S. homoeocarpa	dollar spot	1992	bentgrass/ annual bluegrass	sterol inhibitors[7]

References
1. Chastagner, G.A. and W.E. Vassey. 1982. PlantDisease 66:112-114.
2. Cole, H., B. Taylor and J. Duich. 1968. Phytopathology 58:683-686.
3. Detweiler, A.R., J.M. Vargas, Jr. and T.K. Danneberger. 1983. Plant Disease 67:627-630.
4. Sanders, P.L. 198 Plant Disease 68:776-777.
5. Shane, W.W. and T.K. Danneberger. 1989. Plant Disease 73:775.
6. Vargas, Jr., J.M. 1973. Phytopathology 63:1366-1368.
7. Vargas, Jr., J.M., R. Golembiewski and A.R. Detweiler. 1992. *Golf Course Management* 60(3):50,52,54.
8. Warren, C.G., P.L. Sanders and H. Cole. 1974. Phytopathology 64:1139-1142.

HERBICIDES
(most on agriculture crops; weeds cited pertinent to turf)

Weed	Herbicide	First Report (year)
Lambsquarters	atrazine/simizine	1970
Pigweed	atrazine/simizine	1972
Goosegrass	trifluralin(Treflan)	1973
Annual bluegrass	atrazine/simizine	1976
Barnyardgrass	atrazine/simizine	1978
Annual ryegrass	diclofopmethyl	1982
Annual ryegrass	sulfonylureas	1986
Annual ryegrass	diclofopmethyl	1987

Reference
LeBaron, H.M. 1988. WRCC-60 Meetings, Ciba-Geigy Corp.

TABLE 3.

INSECTICIDES

Insect	Insecticide
Greenbug (Schizaphis graminum)	Chlopyrifos(2)
Southern Chinch Bug (Blissus insularis)	Chlopyrifos(3)
Japanese Beetles (Scarabaeid spp.)	Beniocarb (1)
Southern Chinch Bug	Diazinon (3)

References

1. Ng, Y.S. and S. Ahmad. 1979. Journal Economical Entomology 72:698-700.
2. Niemczyk, H.D. and J.D. Moser. 1982. *in* Advances in Turfgrass Entomology. Piqua, OH.
3. Reinert, J.A. and H.D. Niemczyk. 1982. *in* Advances in Turfgrass Entomology. Piqua, OH.

TABLE 3 (continued).

9

Interspecific Competition

There is no tenure for anyone, not even a species.
— James Lovelock, English scientist

INTERSPECIFIC COMPETITION is the battle between individuals of different species for limited resources. From planting mixed grass species to battling weeds, interspecific competition is the basis of many management decisions.

The ecological principle of competition is that one of two populations of reproducing organisms, if permitted to reproduce, will eliminate the other from the niche. However, as simple as this may seem, outside influences from predators to the environment may modify this outcome so that the species may coexist. Fundamental to the competitive outcome is the relative efficiency with which a species uses its resources as well as the influence of predators.

Principles underlying interspecific competition may be found by looking closely at mixed turfgrass stands. Mixed species stands are common in cool-season turf establishment. For example, improvements in characteristics of perennial ryegrasses make it a more desirable species to use in conjunction with Kentucky bluegrass. Perennial ryegrass is a quick-germinating, vigorous species that provides a needed initial cover and soil stabilization while allowing the slower-germinating Kentucky bluegrass to develop.

From a competitive standpoint, perennial ryegrass has a significant advantage over Kentucky bluegrass by monopolizing resources such as light and nutrients in the initial seedling development stage. The result is zones of resource depletion for the slower Kentucky bluegrass. Niehaus (1976), in investigating the botanical composition of his Kentucky bluegrass / perennial ryegrass mixes, found the percent of Kentucky bluegrass seed by weight was considerably higher than in the established stand. In one combination of "Kenblue" Kentucky bluegrass the amount of seed in the mix exceeded 90 percent, but the actual percentage of Kentucky bluegrass plants in the established stand was 30 percent or less compared to ryegrass. Brede and Duich (1984) found that a Kentucky bluegrass/perennial ryegrass mix with less than 70 percent by weight of Kentucky bluegrass resulted in inadequate establishment of the bluegrass. However, mixes with greater than 95 percent Kentucky bluegrass resulted in poor dispersion of ryegrass and caused unsightly patches.

The use of a companion grass to enhance warm-season turfgrass establishment has provided similar results to those found in Kentucky bluegrass/perennial ryegrass mixes. Vegetatively planting warm-season turfgrasses, either by sprigging or plugging, may take several months before a full canopy cover is achieved. Companion grasses seeded into the vegetatively planted site may provide an initial cover and soil stabili-

Some weeds, such as annual bluegrass, may be either r-selected or K-selected weeds depending on the habitat. In this photograph, annual bluegrass plants have been selected from various habitats; each showing different growth characteristics.

zation until the slower to establish warm-season turfgrass species becomes predominant. Dudeck and Peacock (1986) evaluated the performance of various companion crops in newly plugged St. Augustinegrass and centipedegrass sites. Browntop millet *(Panicum ramosum)* was the most rapid to establish and the most competitive companion crop. Two months after plugging, the amount of St. Augustinegrass and centipedgrass found in plots containing browntop millet was less than the amount of St. Augustinegrass and centipedegrass found in plots plugged alone.

The sequential timing of the seeding of two competing species can have a dramatic outcome on competitive studies. Using perennial ryegrass and fine fescue, King (1971) seeded the species simultaneously at two fertility levels, four weeks apart. When perennial ryegrass was sown first, it's growth was not depressed by competition from the fine fescue. The fertility treatments of nitrogen and phosphorus resulted in a positive growth response for perennial ryegrass. The same was not true for fine fescue which instead exhibited growth inhibition. When fine fescue was seeded first, the same trends were noted but not to the same degree as when perennial ryegrass was seeded first. Competition for nutrients will favor the dominant species, or in this case, the first species to establish. Turfgrass fertilization promotes growth and enhances the aesthetics of the established grasses, but it also discourages competition from invading species such as weeds. Turfgrass fertilization tends to maintain the status quo.

Competition between grass species can occur in its tillers and/or roots. Brede and Duich (1986) looked at competition among perennial ryegrass, an aggressive Kentucky bluegrass cultivar and an annual bluegrass, all established at the same time. The tillering capacity of these grasses was one measurement addressed in their study. Generally, a grass with a high tillering capacity has an advantage over lower tillering grasses (Grime and Hunt, 1975), and Brede and Duich found that annual bluegrass had a greater tillering capacity than perennial ryegrass. Kentucky bluegrass had a tillering capacity less than both annual bluegrass and perennial ryegrass. Seasonal variation did occur with perennial ryegrass having a higher tillering rate in the spring than annual bluegrass, but this finding was reversed in the fall.

Using a partitioning apparatus, Brede and Duich (1986) were able to look at both aboveground and below ground interactions. In instances where competition was restricted to aboveground interactions, Kentucky bluegrass tended to dominate perennial ryegrass. Although Kentucky bluegrass had a lower tillering capacity, its dominance was a result of its ability to sustain consistent growth. Limiting competition to below ground, the perennial ryegrass had a slight advantage.

Overall, the study's findings showed that competition occurred between species even at a short height of cut (slightly above an inch). Additionally, competition existed below ground even when ample quantities of water and nutrients are present. Turfgrass rivalry is an ongoing process even under ideal conditions.

Seasonality, as reflected by the temperature optima for species growth impacts the competitive ability of turfgrass species. As previously mentioned, perennial ryegrass and annual bluegrass tillering capacities change comparatively during the season. In a putting green, the competitive ability of creeping bentgrass and annual bluegrass depends on the time of year. Creeping bentgrass is more competitive in the hotter summer months while annual bluegrass is more competitive in the cooler winter months. Lush (1988) showed that the competitive outcome between creeping bentgrass and annual bluegrass is decided by the tillering capacity of each. In this case, creeping bentgrass was more competitive than annual bluegrass in the summer because of its greater tillering capacity, and not as a result of annual bluegrass plants dying. During the winter, annual bluegrass has a greater tillering capacity making it the dominant species.

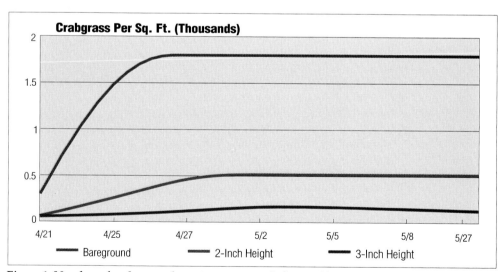

Figure 1. Number of crabgrass plants in an area as influenced by mowing height. (Danneberger, unpublished data)

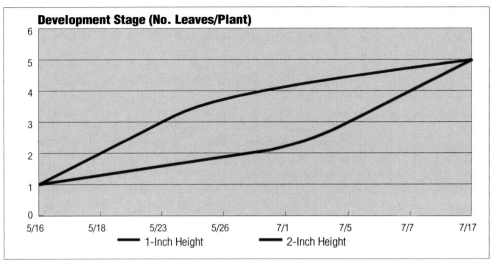

Development Stage (No. Leaves/Plant)

Figure 2. Influence of mowing height on the development of crabgrass. (Danneberger, unpublished data)

The concept described by Grimes and Hunt (1975), and supported by turfgrass studies (Brede and Duich, 1986; Lush, 1988), is that the species with the highest tillering capacity wins even if that capacity is relatively low. For example, in the creeping bentgrass/annual bluegrass competition study, annual bluegrass had a greater capacity to tiller in the summer than in the winter, but because of the creeping bentgrass competition, this capacity was not fully expressed. (Lush, personal communication) In the winter, however, the tillering capacity of annual bluegrass was fully expressed due to the minimal competition from the creeping bentgrass.

SPECIES ADAPTATION: HABITAT INFLUENCE

In Chapter 8, pesticide resistance was shown to occur from selection pressure brought on by the use of pesticides. Habitat also exerts selection pressure on populations of organisms. To survive, plant species that are competing must be able to exploit the weaknesses of any competing organisms. Weeds, which are unwanted plants located in a habitat, provide a good example of interspecific competition in turf. The word "weed" is an interesting term since there is no taxonomic definition because it does not correspond to any single genus or family of plants. However, general characteristics of turfgrass weeds include a difficulty to control in management systems, opportunistic and, when a disturbance to the habitat occurs, they thrive.

In general, two types of weeds occur in turf which predominate under certain habitat conditions. The population growth of the first type of weed is more or less independent of population density. For example, a summer annual weed exposed to a hard freeze will be just as likely to die in a crowded clump of plants as it is growing alone in a bare soil. The second type of weed is density dependent which means the weed's growth rate decreases in the presence of competition. Once the competition eases to a less dense stand, the growth rate may increase. The life history, which is the time period for germination, growth, differentiation and reproduction of these two types of weeds are different.

The life history patterns of these two types of weeds have been described as r and K selecting species. (MacArthur and Wilson, 1967) The r and K denote the parameters from the logistic equation. (Chapter 7) A r-selected weed species is characterized by smaller size, earlier maturity, single reproduction cycle and large reproduction capacity. A K-selected weed species is characterized by a larger size, delayed reproduction, less energy spent for reproduction and a long reproductive cycle.

A K or r species is selected according to the habitat leading Southwood (1977) to suggest a general classification of habitats. From the organism's point of view or in this case the weed's point of view, these habitats are:

Constant - Conditions remain favorable or unfavorable indefinitely.
Seasonal - Regular alternating of favorable and unfavorable conditions.
Unpredictable - Favorable periods of variable duration are interdispersed with periods of unequally unfavorable periods.
Ephemeral - A favorable period is predictively short followed by unfavorable conditions for an indefinite period of time.

A r-selected population is thought to live in either an unpredictable or ephemeral habitat. Under favorable habitat conditions, the population experiences rapid growth, free from competition. However, habitat conditions change unpredictably causing mortality to the population regardless of size or maturity. In K-selecting habitats such as constant or seasonal, conditions are more stable with few unpredictable fluctuations. Under constant or seasonal conditions, a steady population develops resulting in full canopy cover (carrying capacity). Populations under a constant or seasonal habitat undergo severe competition. Under K-selecting conditions, the population size is important with larger individuals being better able to compete. For K-selecting species fewer offspring are produced and less energy is spent on reproductive allocation. Additionally, reproduction is spread over a longer period.

For managing weeds in turf situations, the concept of r-type weeds and K-type weeds is important. Turfgrass weeds that are r-type weeds are typically annuals, but also include a few biennials. The K-type weeds are mostly creeping perennials and some simple perennials. (Table 1) Simple perennials produce relatively high seed numbers. If a void area develops in any turf area, an ideal habitat for r-type weeds is created. Cultural controls that promote a high density discourage the germination and growth of r-type weeds. For example, invasion by foreign plants is most common in bare, thin or weak turf areas caused by biotic (disease, insect) or abiotic (environmental) stresses. Management practices, such as improper mowing, can also contribute to weed infestation. Figure 1 shows the effect mowing height can have on crabgrass (r-selected weed) infestation in a Kentucky bluegrass stand. On a bare soil and at 1-inch height of cut, crabgrass appeared sooner and the number of crabgrass plants were much higher than at the 2-inch height of cut. Additionally, crabgrass development was delayed at the higher mowing height. (Figure 2) From a management standpoint, delaying crabgrass development extends the period for controlling the weed. For example, in situations traditionally calling for an early postemergent herbicide for controlling a weed, the time in which the herbicide can be used is lengthend by the late development.

The K-type weeds present a different problem. They are able to compete in an intense competitive situation making cultural practices that promote turf density less effective. With these weeds, physically removing the weed or chemical treatment is often required.

CASE STUDIES: ANNUAL BLUEGRASSES AND DANDELIONS

Habitats can cause r-type and K-type selections within a speces. Annual bluegrass is a grass species that has developed under both r- and K-type environments. (Law et al, 1977) These researchers collected one type of *poa annua* from large bare areas that had undergone continual disturbance (r-selecting). The second type of annual bluegrass was selected from a permanent pasture (K-selecting). The seeds collected from both types of annual bluegrass were grown from seed in an uncrowded environment. Annual bluegrass from both types were germinated from seed and life histories were measured. The r-selecting annual bluegrasses were smaller in size (Figure 3), and matured earlier as measured from germination to inflorescence production. (Figure 4) In addition, a greater allocation to reproduction by the r-selecting annual bluegrasses lead to a shorter life span. The opposite was true with the K-selecting annual bluegrasses. Annual bluegrass is an extremely difficult weed

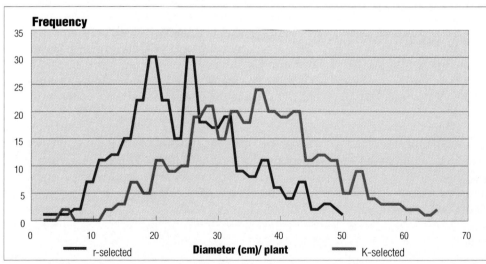

Figure 3. Distribution of diameters for seven months of poa annua plants from a r-selecting environment (opportunistic) and a K-selecting environment. (Data estimated from Law et al, 1977)

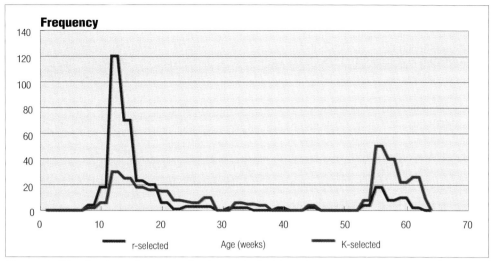

Figure 4. Distribution of prereproductive periods (time from germination to production of inflorescence)for poa annua plants from a r-selecting environment and a K-seleccting environment.

to control in turf since it has the ability to colonize open areas and can be competitive in undisturbed turf situations.

In a similar study with dandelions, Solbrig and Simpson (1974, 1977) identified a number of distinct clones of dandelions via electrophoresis. These clones belonged to one of four biotypes (A-D). Biotype A predominated on a site that was dry, mowed frequently and compacted from foot traffic, while biotype D predominated on a site which was wet, shady, undisturbed and uncompacted. When Solbrig and Simpson collected and seeded the four biotypes and watched them grow under the same environmental conditions, they found that biotype A produced the greatest amount of seeds and produced them earlier while biotype D produced plants that grew big and survived longer. Biotypes B and C, which came from a site that was intermediate between A and D, were intermediate in their reproductive and growth capabilities. Consistent with the previous example, biotype A put most of its resource allocation into reproduction (r-selecting) while biotype D made the least (K-selecting).

LOCALIZED SELECTION DUE TO HABITATS
Management practices can lead to localized habitats which put selection pressure on turf species. Lush (1989) looked at morphological and physiological variations among annual bluegrass populations from a golf course green, fairway and rough. She found that seeds from annual bluegrass plants taken from the green germinated readily while seed from annual bluegrass taken from the fairway and rough needed a chilling period before the seeds germinated. This is a significant difference between two types of annual bluegrass located within yards of each other. When the annual bluegrass plants were allowed to grow up in pots for morphological comparisons, annual bluegrass taken from the green was smaller, slightly more

prostrate, lacked stolons and flowered later compared to annual bluegrass plants from the fairway/rough. From a management perspective, a golf course having a continually germinating annual bluegrass population (golf green) and an annual bluegrass population that requires a dormancy period (golf course fairway), will require different cultural practices for each population. For example, competition from annual bluegrass after core cultivation of a creeping bentgrass fairway in early summer is minimal. However, core

Bermudagrass encroachment into creeping bentgrass is a serious problem for turfgrass managers where both grasses are used. (Courtesy Curt Kause)

cultivation at the same time on a creeping bentgrass green would result in competition from germinating annual bluegrass seeds.

SEEDS AS A SOURCE OF COMPETITION

Seeds are the primary dispersal units of many desirable turfgrass species and their associated weeds. Successful competition depends in part on the inherent ability of seeds to remain dormant in the soil seed bank until conditions become suitable for their germination. Thompson and Grime (1979) classified seeds into four categories based on their release from the mother plant and germination characteristics. These categories were further defined by McDonald et al (1992) as the following:

Type 1: Autumn-germinating species whose transient seed banks are present only throughout the summer; typically, large-seeded grasses which germinate over a wide range of temperature and light conditions. Examples: perennial ryegrass, fescues.

Type 2: Spring-germinating species whose transient seed banks are present only during the winter. Often these have a chilling requirement which imposes winter dormancy; similar to Type 1 in that it is relatively large-seeded and does not requiring light for germination. Example: crabgrass.

Type 3: Species in which most of the seeds germinate soon after they are shed (usually in late summer), but in which a small proportion become incorporated into a persistent seed bank. These species tend to have small seeds which germinate only over a restricted range of temperatures. They often require light. Example: annual bluegrass.

Type 4: Species in which only a few of the seeds germinate soon after dispersal. Most of the seeds enter the persistent seed bank which is large in relation to the annual production. These species differ only in degree from those of Type 3, but represent the extreme case of species in which the seed bank strategy is most strongly developed.

Cool-season turfgrasses tend to be represented in the first three categories, areas which sometimes overlap. The important point is that plants have evolved to fit unique ecological niches while the likelihood of survival is maximized. (McDonald, et al,1992) The key to encouraging desirable turfgrass species or discouraging undesirable weeds from establishing is knowing the conditions that favor each.

Weeds can quickly colonize open or void areas in turf (r-selected types). In most turf soils, the rapid appearance of weeds is the result of a high seed production rate which can result in a potentially large soil seed bank reservoir. (Table 2) For most weeds, germination occurs over a wide temperature range, but some species require light for germination. Some weeds have a dormancy period protecting them from untimely germination triggered by transient favorable weather conditions. (Table 3)

Distribution of weed seeds varies from ecosystem to ecosystem. (Table 4) In situations with little disturbance, such as a well-maintained turfgrass or forest system, the number of weed species is generally smaller than a no-tilled field. No-till farming is not as disruptive to the soil as traditional plowing. Compared to established turfgrass situations, however, no-till is a disruptive practice. Weeds in the disturbed situation tend to be more r-selected types while those from the undisturbed situation tend to be more K-selected. Annual bluegrass, as previously mentioned, can be a r-type or K-type species depending on the environment. Care should be taken when comparing soil seed bank populations with established populations since perennials produce few seeds compared to annuals. Seed bank data may not reflect perennial growth but instead reflect previous annual populations.

Annual bluegrass is a weed of special interest because of its ability to compete against most turfgrass species and its almost ubiquitous nature. Annual bluegrass is a profuse seedhead producer with estimates between 150,000 and 650,000 seeds per meter per year produced. (Lush, 1988a) The abundance of seed, large seed bank and rapid tillering capacity makes it an excellent colonizer of bare areas in turf, especially because unimpeded sunlight enhances germination. Germination of annual bluegrass occurs during the cool moist conditions in the fall with some occurring in the spring. (Beard et al, 1978; Law, 1981)

Contradictory reports exist on necessary conditions for annual bluegrass germination. Seeds collected from Louisiana have a dormancy mechanism that prevents germination at high temperatures, while seeds collected from annual bluegrass in Wisconsin germinated over a wide range of temperatures. (Standifer, 1988) It appears annual bluegrass biotypes in the South have developed a dormancy mechanism while northern seed types germinate more readily. However, differences also occur in a much smaller geographical area. As previously mentioned, Lush (1989) found annual bluegrass growing on a golf green germinated readily while the annual bluegrass from the fairway of the same golf hole required a dormancy (chilling) period.

The soil seed bank of annual bluegrass is divided into two categories: transient and persistent. (Lush, 1988b) The transient bank consists of seeds germinating within a year, and the smaller, persistent seed bank includes seeds not germinating within the same year.

SPACIAL ASPECTS OF COMPETITION

The establishment of high plant populations results in increased mortality through intra- and inter-competition or increased predator (i.e., disease) pressure. Space is an important aspect of the competitive nature of plants in a number of ways including distribution of species and resource partitioning. Dis-

Necrotic ring spot infected Kentucky bluegrass with assorted weeds colonizing the damaged turf.

tribution in space refers to how individuals are clumped or distributed through a habitat. Patterns of dispersion include 1) random in which an equal probability exists for an organism to occupy a space; 2) uniform where individuals tend to avoid other individuals; and 3) in clumps where individuals aggregate or survive in patches. Plants that are patchy in their distribution promote coexistence with competing species. Patchiness may result from disturbances that result in bare or thin areas allowing competitors to germinate. (Bergelson, 1990) For example, necrotic ring spot *(Leptospherea korrea)* causes dead circular patches to occur in a Kentucky bluegrass turf. The dead patch is often colonized by an assortment of weeds.

Unequal spacing between plants causes a large diversity in the number of competing species. Bergelson (1990) found that if annual bluegrass existed in a patchy distribution, the introduction of additional weed species resulted in four to six times more weed seedlings than found in a uniform distributed annual bluegrass turf. This was attributed to the low density of annual bluegrass plants found in the bare areas of the patches. In a uniform annual bluegrass distribution, dying annual bluegrass plants impeded weed seedling development. Thus the prospects for successful introduction of a turfgrass species into an existing turf depend on the species distribution.

PARTITIONING AND COMPOSITION OF RESOURCES

Resource partitioning affects competitive outcomes in mixed species stands. In low maintenance situations, turfgrasses highly competitive for limited resources such as water and nutrients will predominate. Tall fescue is a turfgrass that is able to tap water sources deep in the soil compared to other cool-season turfgrasses due to a deep root system. (Table 5) In a study comparing Kentucky bluegrass and tall fescue under no irrigation and minimal nitrogen applications, the tall fescue turf maintained its uniformity and density. However, the Kentucky bluegrass declined in density, and an invasion of dandelions occurred. (Danneberger, 1990)

In a situation where intermediate levels of water are present, Kentucky bluegrass and tall fescue could coexist in the sense that the bluegrass would compete for the surface moisture while tall fescue draws on deeper moisture sources. Warm-season grasses, as a rule, distribute root systems downward on dry soils to a greater extent than cool-season turfgrasses. (Bennett and Doss, 1960; Doss et al 1960; Evans, 1978; Sheffer et al 1987) Differences can also occur among cultivars of the same species. The root distribution of "Midiron" bermudagrass was more uniform than "U-3" bermudagrass. (Hays et al, 1991) From a management perspective, the "Midiron" mechanism for drought avoidance is enhanced by a uniform root distribution.

The composition of the resource can determine the outcome of a competitive situation. Working with creeping bentgrass sod, Glinski et al (1989) found that the NO_3- should be the predominant nitrogen form compared to NH_4+ when rapid root development is desired. Eggens and Wright (1985) studied the effects of applying nitrogen, in increasing proportions of nitrate to ammonium, to a creeping bent-grass / annual bluegrass stand. (Figure 5) They found that increasing the proportion of nitrate increased the shoot dry weight accumulation of annual bluegrass, but had little effect on the creeping bentgrass. By influencing the available source, in this case nitrogen, the competitive ability of annual bluegrass was enhanced.

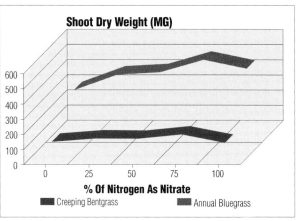

Figure 5. Effect of a nitrogen source on the competitive ability of annual bluegrass and creeping bentgrass. (Eggens and Wright, 1985)

OVERSEEDING WARM-SEASON TURFGRASSES

Overseeding is a unique interspecific competitive situation in which one species is seeded into another. In warm climates where bermudagrass goes dormant, a cool-season turfgrass is seeded into the bermudagrass to provide color; and in golf, an improved playing surface. In addition to the competition that exists between the warm-season grass and the overseeded grass, competition from annual bluegrass in the fall and crabgrass and / or goosegrass in the spring occurs.

Overseeding is done on Southern golf courses and athletic fields with perennial ryegrass, rough bluegrass and creeping bentgrass — the cool-season turfgrasses — acting as the primary overseeding turfgrasses. In the fall, with the onset of cooler temperatures, warm-season grasses such as bermudagrass begin to go dormant. At this time, Southern turfgrass managers overseed with a cool-season grass. In golf course situations, the transition periods during the fall when the bermudagrass is overseeded and again in the spring when the bermudagrass re-initiates growth are often difficult and critical times.

To enhance the chances of a successful overseeding program and to reduce the competitive ability of bermudagrass, turf managers prepare their sites four to six weeks prior to overseeding. Practices such as reducing or eliminating nitrogen fertilization will slow growth, and thatch control will enhance cool-season turfgrass germination. Weed control, primarily annual bluegrass, is important to successful overseeding.

One possible means of reducing the encroachment of bermudagrass into creeping bentgrass is to use a slow growing turfgrass such as zoysiagrass as a buffer. In this case zoysiagrass circles the green and bunker acting as a barrier between creeping bentgrass and the bermudagrass (not visible).

Site preparation activities before seeding vary among turfgrass managers. Common practices include vertical mowing and lowering the mowing height of the bermudagrass. Some managers have tried more extensive practices such as using chemicals to reduce the competitive ability of bermudagrass. However, if any of these activities are too intensive, damage to bermudagrass can occur resulting in a delay in the spring transition back to bermudagrass. (Johnson, 1986; 1987)

Cool-season turfgrasses are overseeded at rates as high as 30 to 35 lbs. per 1,000 square feet of perennial ryegrass. Rough bluegrass and creeping bentgrass are overseeded at lower rates. Blending perennial ryegrass cultivars for overseeding appears to provide no advantage over the use of a single perennial ryegrass cultivar with regard to overall quality. (Krans, 1983)

From a competitive standpoint, the timing of overseeding is critical. If seed is applied too early and warm weather sets in, the bermudagrass will outcompete the new seedlings. If it is too late, the transition will not be smooth with regard to uniformity and color.

Annual bluegrass control consists of applying a preemergent herbicide at least 30 to 60 days before overseeding. (Bingham et al, 1969) However, the control of annual bluegrass is not as effective as an application at the time of overseeding. (Johnson, 1975) The use of postemergent herbicides, such as ethofumesate, have shown good potential for annual bluegrass control applied two to four weeks after overseeding (Johnson, 1988) although, a delay in spring transition from the perennial ryegrass to bermudagrass could occur.

Conversion in the spring back to bermudagrass, especially on putting greens, is a difficult process. During the spring both the perennial ryegrass and bermudagrass are in an active period of growth. Turf managers' attempts at a gradual transition face potential problems. If the transition is too slow, the cool-season turfgrass, especially some of the more heat-tolerant perennial ryegrasses, may retard bermudagrass emergence. Cultural practices such as vertical mowing and core cultivation have been used by turfgrass managers to hasten the spring transition to bermudagrass. In one four-year study, however, the practices of vertical mowing, core cultivation and topdressing had no effect on increasing the rate of bermudagrass coverage in the spring on greens overseeded with perennial ryegrass. (Mazur and Wagner, 1987) In fact, the vertical mowing decreased bermudagrass coverage as well as the turf quality. The use of herbicides and growth regulators have been reported to hasten the transition from perennial ryegrass to bermudagrass. (Johnson, 1988; Mazur, 1988)

CREEPING BENTGRASS (C3) AND BERMUDAGRASS (C4) COMPETITION

Creeping bentgrass is being used on golf course putting greens in the Southern United States. Bermudagrass often surrounds these greens and, in the summer months, can encroach into the creeping bentgrass when it is under stress. From a competitive standpoint, creeping bentgrass during high temperatures is only 50 percent efficient in capturing energy as a warm-season turfgrass. (See Chapter 2, photorespiration)

From a management perspective, the retardation of bermudagrass into a creeping bentgrass turf is a difficult undertaking. Siduron, which is a preemergent annual grass herbicide, has been commonly used with mixed results. Recently, the use of ethofumesate plus the growth regulator flurprimidol, has prevented bermudagrass encroachment to a greater degree than siduron. (Johnson and Carrow, 1989) The effects on bermudagrass with an application of ethofumesate plus flurprimidol, however, diminished in early summer.

Physical removal by hand of bermudagrass from creeping bentgrass is one approach some Southern turfgrass managers use for control. Also, the use of less aggressive warm-season turfgrasses as a buffer between bermudagrass and creeping bentgrass is another approach. For example, the warm-season turfgrass zoysiagrass can be effectively used to compete against bermudagrass. Yet, its ability to encroach into creeping bentgrass is minimal due to the slow rate of growth of zoysiagrass stolons and rhizomes.

PREDICTING COMPETITIVE OUT-COMES: TILMAN'S MODEL

Predicting the outcomes of competitive species is difficult. However, Tilman, an ecologist, has proposed a

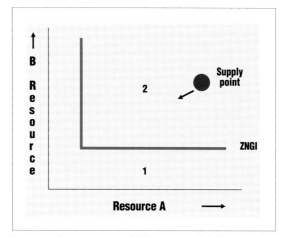

Figure 6. Components of Tilman's model. (See text for explanation.)

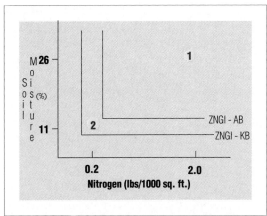

Figure 7. A proposed model for competition between annual bluegrass (AB) and Kentucky bluegrass (KB) with regard to the resources of nitrogen and water at high temperatures (data based on work by Wehner and Atschke, 1981). At high temperatures, annual bluegrass is unable to compete against Kentucky bluegrass at low nitrogen and infrequent irrigation levels.

model for predicting the outcome between species competing for limited resources in a dynamic situation (1986). Tilman's model considers both the dynamics of resource availability as well as the competing individuals (same or different species). Tilman's model has not been applied to turf, and subsequently not tested in a turf situation. Yet, the concept provides a novel means of looking at turfgrass competition.

Tilman's model is built upon the concept that each species has a minimum requirement for each resource, similar to the boundaries that define a species niche. In Tilman's model, a line is drawn to represent the minimum level of a resource needed for growth which he calls the zero net growth isoline (ZNGI). (Figure 6) Below the ZNGI for each resource, in this case represented by A and B, the species cannot survive. Above the ZNGI line in the case of resource A, or to the right of the ZNGI for resource B, growth and development may occur. The level of the resources is represented by the supply point. The supply point identifies the level of each resource at a given time. As the species consumes the resource, the supply point moves toward the origin but in a diagonal direction toward a ZNGI. (Actual movement is determined mathematically by vector analysis.) If the resources are replenished, the supply point moves toward location 2 of Figure 6. A critical concept for this model is that each species have different resource requirement levels. If the supply point drops to a level that it is at point 1 in Figure 6, the species cannot survive since it is outside the area of growth defined by the ZNGI.

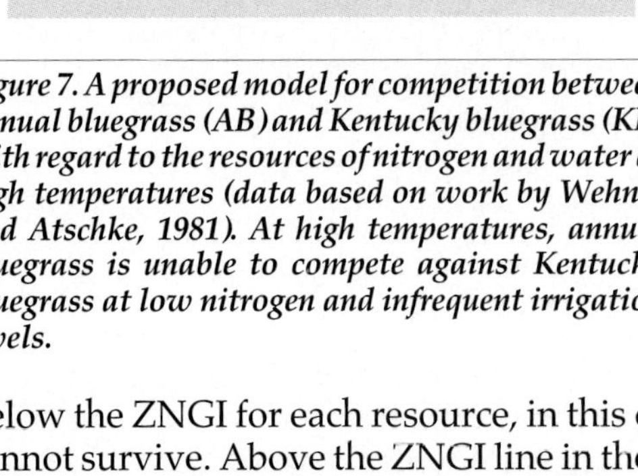

Using Tilman's model for competition between species, two outcomes can occur. The first is the competitive exclusion principle where the

Figure 8. In this competition model, annual bluegrass (AB) will be competitively excluded given creeping bentgrass (CB) tolerance to lower levels of these resources.

ZNGI for one species lies below that of the competing species. For example, using the resources moisture and nitrogen, a competitive model of annual bluegrass and Kentucky bluegrass may be proposed. The model is based on work previously decribed in Chapter 5. (Wehner and Watschke, 1981) During periods of high temperature stress, high nitrogen levels and frequent applications of water minimizes any competitive advantage Kentucky bluegrass has over annual bluegrass. However, at low nitrogen levels and infrequent irrigation, Kentucky bluegrass will be

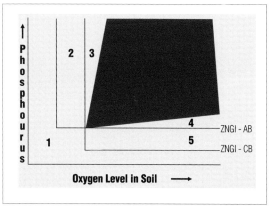

Figure 9. Overlapping niche requirements of annual bluegrass (AB) and creeping bentgrass (See text for explanation).

more competitive than annual bluegrass during periods of high temperature stress. This relationship between Kentucky bluegrass and annual bluegrass is shown in Figure 7. At supply point 1 (high moisture and nitrogen levels) annual bluegrass and Kentucky bluegrass coexist. However, as the resources are drawn down (resource point 2), Kentucky bluegrass is much more competitive and will likely exclude annual bluegrass from the habitat if temperatures remain high during a prolonged period.

Another example of competitive exclusion is the competition of annual bluegrass and creeping bentgrass for nutrients. Using data trends from Waddington et al, (1978) on the effects of phosphorus and potassium in annual bluegrass/creeping bentgrass rivalry, a competitive exclusion model is proposed. (Figure 8) In this example, if the supply point is at 1, neither annual bluegrass (AB) nor creeping bentgrass (CB) will survive. If the initial resource point is at point 3, both AB and CB coexist. However, as the resource point is drawn down to point 2, CB will survive and effectively exclude AB which is below its own ZNGI point.

The second outcome of Tilman's model reveals that if two species compete for resources that are differentially limiting to each, niche overlap can occur. Using work by Youngner (1959) and Waddington et al, (1978), a niche overlap model has been sketched. (Figure 9) Annual bluegrass is particularly limited by low phosphorus while creeping bentgrass is limited by low oxygen in the soil. The oxygen level reflects the degree of soil compaction; the lower the oxygen level the greater the compaction. If the supply point is located in region 1, neither annual bluegrass nor creeping bentgrass will survive since the point is below ZNGI for both species. In region 2 — the supply point — the oxygen level is below the ZNGI for creeping bentgrass but above the ZNGI for annual bluegrass. At this point annual bluegrass will exclude creeping bentgrass. In region 3, the oxygen level is likely to be severely limiting to creeping bentgrass resulting in annual bluegrass outcompeting and excluding creeping bentgrass from the habitat. If the supply point is located in region

135

5, the phosphorus level is below that required for annual bluegrass survival. In this instance, creeping bentgrass will exclude annual bluegrass. In region 4, creeping bentgrass will still exclude annual bluegrass. If the supply point is located in the gray area, neither species has a competitive advantage resulting in a state of coexistence. The level of coexistence depends on the relative need for a limiting resource. The Tilman model allows for changing resource supplies (supply point), but disturbance effects are not considered.

From a turfgrass manager's point of view, it is difficult to determine the supply point location and which turfgrass is more competitive with a depleting resource. However, turf managers need to be concerned when they are using a resource to influence a plant community makeup by limiting water, reducing fertility, etc. An important aspect to remember is that a point is eventually reached in which the growth of either or all desired species is no longer promoted.

Common r-Type and K-Type Weeds of Turfgrasses

r - type	K - type
Crabgrass	Dandelion
Knotweed	White clover
Spurge	Buckhorn plantain
Ragweed	Wild violet
Pigweed	Ground ivy
Foxtail	Speedwells
Barnyardgrass	
Goosegrass	
Dandelion	

TABLE 1.

Number of Seeds Produced by a Single Weed Plant

Weed	Life cycle	Reproduce mainly by	Number of seeds/plant
Barnyardgrass	A	seed	7,160
Lambsquarters	A	seed	72,450
Prostrate Pigweed	A	seed	14,600
Purslane	A	seed	52,300
Sandbur	A	seed	1,110
Black Medic	A/P	seed	2,350
Knotweed	A	seed	6,380
Yellow Woodsorrel	A/P	seed	570
Yellow Nutsedge	P	seed/tubers	2,420
Red Sorrel	P	seed/rhizome	250
Broadleaf Plantain	P	seed	36,150
Curly Dock	P	seed	29,500
Thistle	P	seed/rhizome	680

TABLE 2.   A = annual, P = perennial   *(Source: O.A. Stevens, 1932)*

136

Conditions Favorable for Weed Seed Germination

Common Weed Name	Life Cycle*	Germination Requirements, Temperature	Light	Comments
Annual bluegrass	A-P	wide range	(2C-35C)	beneficial
Barnyardgrass	A	20/30 C (alt.)	needed	
Broadleaf plantain	P	wide range	essential	dormancy period required
Buckhorn plantain	P	20/30 C (alt.)	inconclusive	prechill beneficial to germination
Chickory	P	20/30 C (alt.)	beneficial	
Canada thistle	P	20 C	beneficial to young seeds	
Common chickweed	A	20/30 C (alt.)	——	soil stimulates germination of re-cently harvested seeds
Dandelion	P	wide range	beneficial at high temperatures	no dormancy
Goosegrass	A	20 to 35 C	beneficial (needed at high temperatures)	
Lambsquarter	A	20 C	not required	dormancy period required
Large crabgrass	A	10 to 25 C	beneficial	prechill a require-ment
Mouse-ear chickweed	P	20/30 C (alt.)	——	
Prostrate Pigweed	A	25 to 35 C	periodic (red or white)	
Purple Nutsedge	P	20(dark)/30 (light)C		tubers/seeds
Red Sorrel	P	20/30 C (alt.)	required	
Smooth crabgrass	A	20 to 35 C	not required	prechill is a require-ment
Yellow Foxtail	A	20/30 C (alt.)	——	freshly harvested seeds dormant
Yellow Nutsedge	P	10 C		tubers major pro-pagation unit
Yellow Rocket	A	20 to 30 C	needed	

TABLE 3.   *A = annual; P = perennial; alt. = alternating

Weed Seeds Present in the Soil Under Three Different Ecosystems

Weed Seed	Common Name	No-till farming	Forest	Bentgrass turf
		— seeds/acre at 3-inch depth (in millions) —		
Armanthus spp.	Pigweed	23.835	6.81	—
Brassica rapa	Wild Mustard	1.135	—	—
Chenopodium album	Lambsquarter	13.62	38.59	9.08
Cichorium intybus	Chicory	1.135	—	—
Cirsium arvense	Canada Thistle	1.135	—	—
Datura stranmonium	Jimson Weed	1.135	—	—
Digitaria spp.	Crabgrass spp.	1.135	—	—
Echinochloa crus-galli	Barnyardgrass	2.270	—	—
Hordeum jubatum	Foxtail Barley	1.135	—	—
Panicum dichotomiflorum	Fall Panicum	1.135	—	—
Phalaris arundinacea	Reed Canarygrass	1.135	—	—
Plantago lanceolata	Common Buckhorn	—	—	2.27
Plantago major	Broadleaf Plantain	1.135	—	13.62
Poa annua	Annual Bluegrass	—	—	29.51
Polygonium convolvulus	Wild Buckwheat	1.135	—	—
Polygonium pensylvanicum	Smartweed	2.270	—	—
Portulaca oleracea	Purslane	24.97	18.16	6.81
Rumex crispus	Curly Dock	1.135	—	—
Setaria viridus	Green Foxtail	9.080	—	—
Solonum ptycanthum	Eastern Black Nightshade	1.135	—	—
Stellaria media	Chickweed	38.59	—	—
Trifolium repens	White Clover	1.135	—	—
Urtica dioica	Stinging Nettle	1.135	—	—

(Source: E. Regnier)

TABLE 4.

Root Distribution of Five Cool-Season Turfgrasses by Depth

Depth (inches)	Kentucky bluegrass	Perennial ryegrass	Tall fescue	Creeping bentgrass	Annual bluegrass
		%			
0-4	75	33	35	42	100
4-8	20	28	34	41	—
8-12	5	29	23	17	—
>12	-	10	8	-	—

(Source: A.J. Koski)

TABLE 5.

10

Predator Disturbances

Man is but a reed, the most feeble thing in nature; but
he is a thinking reed. — Blaise Pascal, French mathematician

DISTURBANCES OCCUR continually in plant communities. These disruptions range from rare events such as earthquakes, fires and hurricanes to common microenvironmental events such as a raindrop hitting a seed. Major biotic disturbances in turfgrass systems stem from the many organisms feeding upon turfgrasses.

Predators of plants include insects, pathogens, animals, parasitic plants and man. Even mowers can be considered predators. Mowing affects turf similarly to animals grazing on a pasture or grassland. Predators are described as either selective or non-selective. Selective predators differentially affect plant communities because they choose a small group of species among a diversity of species to attack. Non-selective predators attack plants with little, if any, selectivity. Although a non-selective predator such as a mower may "graze" indiscriminately, the results may diferentially affect the various plant species.

MOWING, A NON-SELECTIVE PREDATOR

Mowing is a direct effect of man's intervention into an ecological system. In general ecological terms, this tampering moves the turf system into suboptimal conditions. In domestic turf, however, mowing is a necessary practice to give it the desired aesthetic and utilitarian characteristics.

Possible consequences of mowing include: increased susceptibility of tall growing plants to injury over low growing plants, the possible elimination of a weak or poorly adapted species brought on by the stress of mowing and the creation of a site opening to colonization by other species.

Charles Darwin was the first to observe and report the effects a non-selective predator has on a turfgrass community. In "The Origin of Species by Means of Natural Selection (1859)," Darwin observed:

> *"If turf which has long been mown (the case would be the same with turf closely*
> *browsed by quadrupeds) be let to grow, the most vigorous plants gradually kill the*

less vigorous, though fully grown plants. Thus out of 20 species growing on a little plot of mown turf, nine species perished from the other species being allowed to grow up freely."

In turf, mowing can act as the driving force to either eliminate a subordinate species from a site or cause an increase in diversity. Mowing effects are aptly demonstrated in a mixed stand of Kentucky bluegrass and annual bluegrass. Kentucky bluegrass is a subordinate species when competing with annual blue-grass at low mowing heights. As the height of cut is decreased below the optimum for Kentucky bluegrass, its competitive ability compared to annual bluegrass is low. Turgeon and Vargas (1980) showed that in a space of a few years a low cutting height will convert a nearly 100 percent Kentucky bluegrass turf to a predominantly annual bluegrass stand. (Table 1)

Management intervention via improved cultivar selection may increase the competitive ability of Kentucky bluegrass. (Table 1) Turgeon and Vargas found that when lowering the mowing height on a common type of Kentucky bluegrass cultivar, "Kenblue," a significant increase in the annual bluegrass population occurred. An improved Kentucky bluegrass cultivar, "A-20," mowed at a more adaptive mowing height (1.5 inches) was effective in excluding annual bluegrass from the turf. At the lower mowing height, annual bluegrass invaded A-20, but not to the same extent as Kenblue. Kenblue, as most common types of Kentucky bluegrass cultivars, has an upright growth habit (tall plant) and suffers most from continued mowing at a shorter height than a low growing plant such as annual

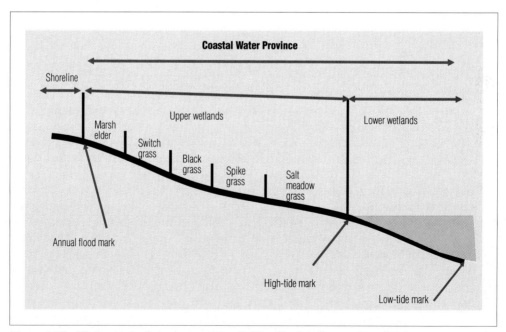

Figure 1. The likely vegetative components of a New England coastal wetland.

140

bluegrass. If conditions are favorable for annual bluegrass, competitive exclusion occurs. However, if a more prostrate Kentucky bluegrass cultivar is used, such as A-20, its ability to survive is greater, yet it still suffers from low mowing height resulting in some annual bluegrass invasion. Cultivar improvements have made turfgrasses more competitive with regard to mowing. (Sheffer et al, 1978)

Older turfgrass cultivars and pasture types are genetically predisposed to less biomass per area than newer cultivars when mowed at a set height. (Lush, 1992) Newer cultivars tolerate closer "neighbors" better and form biomass by packing more plants of a given height into a given area. Older cultivars given their lower biomass, provide more open spaces for weeds to invade.

The timing of mowing influences community makeup in newly established turfs. Brede and Brede (1988) working with a tall fescue/annual ryegrass mix found that annual ryegrass composition in the stand was greatly reduced if the mix was closely clipped three days after emergence. If the mowing was delayed for six weeks, the annual ryegrass predominated.

In some instances mowing is so severe that normal competition between individual species becomes relatively unimportant. This is described as "exploiter-mediated coexistence." (Begon, M. et al, 1990) This situation is common on short-cut putting greens. If the creeping bentgrass is cut below an optimum height, the stand density decreases which in turn allows for weed invasion. Continued low mowing also reduces the competitive ability of weeds to the point that they are unable to crowd out the existing creeping bentgrass. As a result, a situation forms in which neither the creeping bentgrass nor the weeds are able to dominate the site causing coexistence.

The effects of mowing heights on the competitive ability of both annual bluegrass and creeping bentgrass have been demonstrated experimentally. Paclobutrazol (O.M. Scotts TGR[R]) is a plant growth regulator that is used to differentially suppress annual bluegrass in creeping bentgrass turf. Following treatment, creeping bentgrass literally grows over the top of the annual bluegrass. Research conducted at a height of cut of 0.5 inch with Paclobutrazol has resulted in very pronounced creeping bentgrass encroachment, almost to the point of excluding annual bluegrass. (Table 2) However at a 0.125 inch height of cut little, if any, encroachment occurs. The low mowing height reduces the effectiveness of the PGR by eliminating the competitive ability of creeping bentgrass.

Mowing frequency affects turfgrass health. Madison (1962) found that daily mowing of creeping bentgrass resulted in greater density and smaller plants. With less frequent mowing, this relationship did not hold true. On Kentucky bluegrass, frequent mowing (two mowings per week) with clippings returned to the soil resulted in higher quality turf than weekly or biweekly mowing. (Haley et al, 1985) In general, very frequent mowing has a detrimental effect on turfgrass plants including reduced wear tolerance. On putting greens, however, less frequent mowing may result in a reduction in putting green speed. (Radko et al, 1981) Sharpness of the mower blades plays an important role in mowing effects on turfgrasses. Steinegger et al (1983) found that mowing Kentucky bluegrass with dull blades resulted in lower turfgrass quality, increased susceptibility to leaf spot disease and greater gasoline consumption. However, they did not find that the wounding caused by dull blades resulted in any change in the energy efficiency of the turf as measured by water use.

SELECTIVE PREDATORS...PESTS

In an ecological sense, stability is indicated by the tendency of the species to remain at the same frequency. The stability is provided by an intricate system of checks and balances. In other words, pests reach a balance with their surroundings that allows for some damage, but unchecked pest growth resulting in excessive damage is highly unlikely. A pure ecologist has no favorites; pests do not exist. All organisms have a place within an ecosystem even if two or more organisms share the same "rung" on the ladder. In turf, we define a pest as an organism that disrupts the aesthetic or functional characteristics of the turf.

Turfgrass expectations determine the number of pests that are a concern. On turf used in highway situations, pests are considered of minor importance while on a putting green, pests may be a major problem. Although a greater concern on putting greens, the actual number of turfgrass pests is higher on highway turf. (Bottom photo courtesy of Mike Koetzer)

The cultural intensity of a turf defines a pest. This is most obvious in comparing a high maintenance turf such as a creeping bentgrass putting green vs. a highway roadside. In a putting green situation where a uniform, one grass species (monoculture) is desired, the number of organisms perceived as pests (weeds, pathogens, insects) is high. In a roadside situation where a turf cover is desired, but the species makeup is secondary in importance, the actual number of organisms that are thought to be pests may actually be greater than on the putting green, but less significant. Given the expectation of the roadside turf, pest management is minimal to non-existent. The first step in developing a pest management strategy is to determine the expectations for a turf, followed by the identification of the organisms considered to be pests.

PEST MANAGEMENT STRATEGIES

Over the years a revolution in the quality and quantity of managed turf has occurred. In the early part of the 20th century, turf quality was governed in large part by the weather, luck and the ability of a manager through cultural practices to minimize pests. Chemical control of pests was less sophisticated with the use of relatively toxic, broad-spectrum products such as lead arsenate, sulfur, iron sulfate and other such chemicals for weed, insect and fungi control. The result was a relatively low quality of turf achieved through few inputs.

With the discovery of DDT in 1939 followed by the hormone 2,4-D in 1944, a revolution in chemical control of pests occurred. With these and other discoveries the use of pesticides during the 1950s and early 1960s skyrocketed. It was as if the secret to turfgrass management and agriculture in general could be found in a bottle. The elimination of competing organisms or pests resulted in quality and functional improvements in turf. But as with the concern worldwide over the environmental impact of DDT then, and later on a much smaller scale, the concept of integrated pest management (IPM) evolved.

In strict terms, pest management is an ecological matter. (Flint and van den Bosch, 1981) In attempting to minimize turf damage from pests, whether by cultural or chemical methods, it should be done with minimal disturbance to the ecosystem. The essence of IPM is to provide the desired quality with minimal ecological, economical and sociological consequences. From a practical point of view, IPM consists of monitoring the pest and developing management strategies against those pests. Monitoring environmental conditions is critical. This requires the turfgrass manager to identify the pests of concern, determine the level of pest intrusion and monitor weather conditions where appropriate (i.e., are conditions favorable for pathogen infection) and then correlate these two together to develop an effective management program.

Resistant cultivars and cultural measures will always be the backbone of pest management. Biological agents are being tested but results are currently inconclu-

sive. Thus, along with resistant cultivars and cultural measures, pesticides will continue to be important to the production of high quality turf for the near future.

In nature a dynamic relationship exists between a host plant and a pathogen. Over time as the host and pathogen evolve side by side, a give and take occurs. As a virulent strain of the pathogen occurs it breaks down the resistance of the host until a buildup of resistant host individuals occurs with a subsequent reduction in the virulent population.

Changes in pathogen virulence must be continually balanced by changes in host resistance. This evolutionary process between virulence of the pathogen and resistance by the plant host is described by the gene for gene theory originally demonstrated by Flor (1971). The concept is that for each gene(s)

An important aspect of integrated pest management (IPM) is the monitoring of the pest. In this photograph, an entomologist is applying a solution containing water and dish washing liquid to the turf. Any insects that are in the turf will be driven to the surface by the solution. This provides a means of monitoring some turfgrass insect pests.

that may convey resistance in the plant, the pathogen has a corresponding virulent gene(s). The resistant gene in the host can be detected only by the corresponding virulent gene in the pathogen and vice versa. When a new virulent strain of the pathogen appears, the resistance of the host is lost. Plant breeders can condense the time it takes nature to overcome the new virulent strain by introducing a resistant gene; thus the development of a resistant cultivar. The gene for gene concept has not been proven in turfgrasses because of the number of genes present that convey general resistance. It is, however, presumed to apply.

To expand the genetic diversity of a turfgrass population, blending multiple cultivars of a species is widely practiced. The rationale is that if one cultivar falls prey to a disease, the remaining cultivar(s) will fill in. Selection of the proper blend is paramount to achieving the desired result. For example, Vargas and Turgeon (1980) found that blending a susceptible Kentucky bluegrass cultivar with a melting-out resistant cultivar did not result in dominance by the resistant cultivar. They postulated that the susceptible cultivar allowed for such an inoculum buildup that the resistant cultivar was also adversely affected. However, over a longer time period and in instances of less intense disease pressure, dominance may prevail.

The necessity in blending cultivars is dependent on the propagation method. (Sweeney and Danneberger, 1993) Cultivars that are produced apomictically (asexual reproduction, each seed is identical to the mother) or vegetatively usually consist of a single genotype. Blending cultivars of Kentucky bluegrass which are apomictic is strongly recommended to increase genetic diversity.

On the other hand, the production of seed from a sexual cross results in a number of different genotypes among the progeny unless both the male and female parents are homozygous. In species that are predominantly self-pollinating, homozygosity is relatively easy to achieve and maintain. Many turfgrass species are cross pollinators, however, and achieving homozygosity is impractical and uneconomical in these cases.

Since a single superior heterozygous genotype cannot be reproduced exactly via sexual reproduction, several superior genotypes are selected and intermated to form a synthetic variety. A synthetic variety consists of a number of unique individuals that share many characteristics of the selected parents.

Although any individual in the population cannot be reproduced exactly by sexual seed production the population itself, with its unique proportion of genes, is reproducible by intermating the original parents or vegetative clones of the parents. (Table 5)

An example of asexual vs. sexual reproduction effects on a turfgrass species

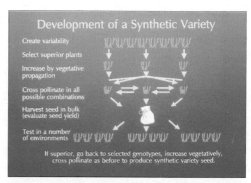

The genetic diversity of turfgrass populations is enhanced by blending multiple cultivars of a species with the idea that one variety will fill in for another should a disease outbreak occur.

Pheromone traps may provide a means of monitoring flying insects such as the black cutworm moth. (Courtesy David Shetlar)

is found in creeping bentgrass. In the early 1980s, bacterial wilt *(Xanthomonas compestris var. graminis)* was found to be a devastating disease that was host specific to "Toronto" creeping bentgrass, a vegetatively propagated variety. However, this disease has not been found on the synthetic creeping bentgrass cultivars such as "Penncross," most likely because of the inherent genetic diversity found in the seed population.

Many cultural controls reduce the risk or level of disease. These practices may consist of proper watering, fertilization or mowing. Cultural practices act to slow down the development of the pathogen in the infected plant. (Chapter 7)

PESTICIDES

Pesticides are compounds that kill pests. Pesticides are derived from a number of sources including inorganic, botanical, microbial, biological and synthetic. (Table 3) Strictly speaking, organic compounds include carbon and can be of biological or non-biological origin. The botanical pesticides are derived naturally from plants and are used in the area of insect control. Microbial pesticides are compounds derived from microbial organisms. Biological controls include using parasites, predators or pathogens to manage pests. Biological control agents are not widely used for weed or disease control. However, research at Cornell University (Nelson, 1990) has shown some beneficial suppression of dollar spot and brown patch with certain composts and organic fertilizers. This may be due to the presence of antagonistic organisms. And as previously mentioned in Chapter 6, some antagonistic organisms may prove to be effective biological controls for some turfgrass diseases.

Milky Spore Disease, caused by the bacteria *Bacillus popilliae*, may be an effective biological control agent of Japanese beetle. The bacteria is consumed by the grub and multiplies, literally filling the grub and causing death. After death, the spores are released making them available in the soil for other grubs. Several disadvantages to Milky Spore are that it is only effective on Japanese beetle grubs and it requires a few years to build up to an effective dose in the soil. However, once populations are established, yearly control will be achieved without subsequent applications. Recently, variable results with the milky spore disease has been reported.

An exciting new biological control for insects is the use of certain non-pathogenic nematodes that infect a range of turfgrass insects. These nematodes promise to be a future means of insect management. (Shetlar et al, 1988)

A recent study found that the conversion of a fungal plant pathogen to a non-pathogenic, endophyte strain conveyed disease resistance to the pathogenic strain and other plant pathogens. (Freeman and Rodriquez, 1993) In this study, the

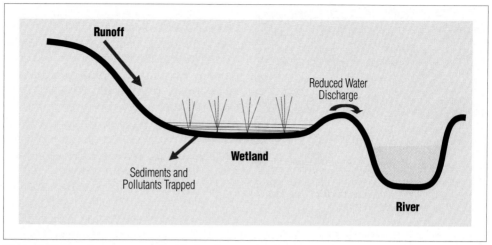

Figure 2. Wetlands serve as a valuable flood control and water treatment facility for contaminated runoff.

researchers introduced a mutant strain of a virulent pathogen that did not cause disease. The mutant strain was able to grow and develop within the plant, and when the plant was challenged with a known virulent strain, no disease occurred. The ramifications of the development of mutants as biocontrol agents may have a considerable impact on pest management in the future.

SYNTHETIC PESTICIDES

Synthetic compounds are man-made products. Since the beginning of turf management, these products have received the greatest attention in pest control. As a result, synthetic compounds have been developed to control insects, weeds and pathogens with a great deal of success. (See Appendixes E, F and G for chemical listings.)

Synthetic pesticides by their nature are relatively non-selective. In other words, pesticides are lethal to both target and non-target organisms. Beneficial predators may succumb to the same fate as their turf destroying cohorts. Pesticide effects on soil organisms are variable depending on the organism. Research has shown a 60 percent reduction in insect populations following an insecticide application to a Kentucky bluegrass lawn. (Cockfield and Potter, 1983) In highly maintained turfs treated with pesticides and fertilizers, predatory insects are less diverse and abundant than in untreated sites. (Cockfield and Potter, 1985; Arnold and Potter, 1987) Additionally, beneficial insect predator populations can be suppressed for a significant period of time after a pesticide application. (Cockfield and Potter, 1984)

Pesticides may alter the growth of turfgrass plants and increase the severity of pests not targeted. Certain herbicides may reduce root growth, shoot growth and enhance thatch formation. In addition, the herbicides bensulide and benefin have been shown to slightly increase the severity of brown patch and dollar spot on bermudagrass and Pythium blight on perennial ryegrass. (Karr et al, 1979) Smiley

(1981), in a review on pesticide non-target effects, reported greater incidence of the patch diseases and stripe smut with bandane applications.

Pesticides may act directly by influencing the capacity of the pathogens for growth or host resistance, or the balance between pathogenic fungi and other organisms. (Smiley, 1981) Fungicide applications to control one pathogen may enhance the severity of others. Benzimidazole fungicides are used on a wide spectrum of pathogens. However, these fungicides have little activity on *Pythium spp.*, increasing the potential for *Pythium* blight in situations where benzimidazole fungicides are overused. (Warren et al, 1976) Similiar effects were found when the severity of red thread on perennial ryegrass was increased with repeated applications of benomyl. (Dernoeden et al, 1985)

Not all non-target effects are detrimental. Fungicide applications have been reported to increase the quality of perennial ryegrass and Kentucky bluegrass. (Dernoeden et al, 1985; Kane and Smiley, 1983) Fungicides used to control red thread and stripe smut were shown to indirectly control crabgrass. (Dernoeden, 1989; Dernoeden and Krouse, 1990) Certain sterol inhibiting fungicides have also been reported to enhance seedling root and shoot growth. (Goatley and Schmidt, 1990) On Kentucky bluegrass sod, the sterol inhibiting fungicides propiconazole and triademifon enhanced post-transplant rooting and sod strength. (Goatley and Schmidt, 1991) These stimulation effects are most likely rate and timing dependent since Kane and Smiley (1983) have reported suppressed root and shoot growth with similar fungicides at higher rates.

Monitoring the weather to determine if environmental conditions are favorable for pest activity, especially disease development, is an important aspect of integrated pest management. Shown here is a turfgrass disease predictor which monitors environmental conditions to determine if a disease outbreak is probable. (Courtesy Neogen Corp.)

Pesticide effects on soil microorganisms is of minor importance. (Greaves, 1987) Recent research on sequential pesticide applications has shown that the effects on the microbial population are short-lived. (Schuster and Schroder, 1990) Soil microorganisms play a beneficial role in the breakdown of pesticides. With any number of chemicals microorganisms are able to take toxic materials and break them down into harmless compounds. The structure of the compound does influence the breakdown rate. For instance, 2,4-D is rapidly broken down, but the addition of a chlorine molecule (2,4,5-T) is resistant to microbial breakdown for a longer period of time.

A pesticide that is applied repeatedly causing a comparatively rapid decomposition rate than the same pesticide applied on a non-repeated site, is said to have enhanced degradation. What happens in soils where enhanced degradation has been detected is that microorganisms have found a means of using a pesticide molecule as a source of carbon resulting in a quick degradation that would not normally occur. The result is a substantial reduction in the efficacy of the product. Enhanced degradation is not widely documented on turf, but has occurred with some commonly used turf pesticides on other agriculture crops. (Table 4)

Strategies for minimizing the likelihood of enhanced degradation involve using good management practices including:

* Using cultural practices that minimize the need for pesticide use. This includes practices such as proper nitrogen programs to minimize common turf diseases, and maintaining a high density lawn to reduce the probability of weed invasion.
* Use pesticides sparingly; only when needed. This can include checking for the presence of an insect before spraying, or spraying for disease only when environmental conditions are favorable.
* Apply pesticides only at proper rates, and beware of formulation effects. Some research has found that herbicides formulated as a granular are less susceptible to degradation than liquid sprays. (Osgerby, 1973)

Research with herbicides has shown that by adding an extender (chemical that extends the longevity of the herbicide), the persistence of a herbicide in the presence of degrading organisms can be lengthened. (Obrigawitch et al, 1983) If enhanced degradation becomes a major problem, cultural practices and new types of formulation are alternatives turf managers can implement.

In summary, synthetic pesticides are a significant component in high maintenance turfgrass situations. Efficient use of these compounds can result in an aesthetic and functional turf. However, overuse or incorrect application rates can lead to detrimental non-target effects.

WETLANDS DISTURBANCE: A SPECIAL NOTE

No environmental issue in recent times has caused as much public uproar and has been so politically charged as that of the wetlands. What defines a wetland and what does not can make the difference between whether a golf course, a housing subdivision or a commercial property gets built. Since landscaping and turf maintenance are integral parts of golf course, housing and commercial properties, the wetlands issue is of major concern. It is estimated that since 1780, more than 50 percent of the wetlands in the continental United States have been lost. The draining of wetlands for agricultural and commercial development are the major causes behind disappearing wetlands. Wetlands are fragile ecological systems that cannot survive any form of human excavation, grading and filling.

Wetlands are areas that undergo flooding at least once a year for a period of time. Legally defined, however, wetlands — as stated by the "Federal Manual for Delineating Wetlands" — is not clear. Yet, a wetland is judged to be based on three parameters: hydrology, vegetation and soils. What makes a wetland is the presence of water.

Hydrophytic vegetation describes plants that live in "wet" conditions. Figure 1 shows a typical New England seashore wetland with a succession of vegetation occurring further inland. However, plants by themselves are not necessarily an

Turfgrasses may coexist with sensitive environmental areas, such as wetlands, if care is taken.

indication of a wetland since the majority of wetland plants also grow in non-wetland areas.

Wetlands typically possess hydric soils which are saturated, flooded or ponded long enough during the growing season to develop anaerobic conditions in the upper profile. Hydric soils alone, however, does not necessarily mean the area is a wetland. Ecologically, wetlands are important at population, ecosystem and global levels. At the population level, wetlands are a home to waterfowl, fish, shellfish, animals, timber and other vegetation, as well as endangered species. More than 30 percent of endangered species are tied to wetlands.

From an ecosystem view, wetlands are important in flood mitigation, storm abatement, water quality and aesthetics. Wetlands are able to reduce the impact of water runoff by slowing the rate of discharge and spreading it over a longer period of time. (Figure 2) The quality of water is greatly enhanced as it moves into a wetland and is ultimately discharged. The flow of contaminated water into the wetlands may be immobilized by microbial and plant activity, physically filtered through absorption or deposition and/or chemically inactivated by oxidation and other reactions. The effect of wetlands on water quality is the reason the Environmental Protection Agency under The Clean Air and Water Act is so involved in wetlands regulation. In addition to water quality, wetlands also are aesthetically pleasing to a segment of the population.

The global value of wetlands is found in the cycling of major elements. Wetlands are an integral part of the nitrogen cycle with a considerable amount of denitrification occurring. Wetlands are involved in the cycling of sulfur. The anaerobic situation present in wetlands results in the formation of hydrogen sulfide. In addition, wetlands serve as a large source of carbon.

What effects the draining of the large wetlands in Canada, Alaska and Siberia have on the release of carbon dioxide to the atmosphere, thus magnifying the greenhouse effect is worth pondering.

Effects of Mowing Heights and Fertilization Rates on the Percent of Annual Bluegrass in Selected Kentucky Bluegrass Cultivars

Mowing Height	1.5 inches				0.75 inches			
N fertility (lbs/M/year)	2	4	6	8	2	4	6	8
Cultivar	------------ %annual bluegrass --------							
Kenblue	25	35	40	50	60	75	80	100
Merion	13	5	3	15	15	25	35	45
A-20	0	0	0	0	12	5	5	10

TABLE 1.   *(Source: Selected and estimated from Turgeon and Vargas, 1980)*

Paclobutrazol Effectiveness for Controlling Annual Bluegrass in a Creeping Bentgrass Turf at Two Mowing Heights

Rate	Application Timing	0.5 inch cut % poa annua	0.125 inch cut %poa annua
light	spring	4	27
normal	spring	6	23
light	spring-fall	10	32
normal	spring-fall	3	28
light	fall	5	30
normal	fall	7	28
untreated		20	40

TABLE 2.   *(Source: J.R. Street)*

note: applications made the spring of 1988 with readings taken in May, 1989

Various Pesticides Used to Control Pests

Classification	Examples	Comments
Inorganics	Common salts	used as a herbicide
	Chlorates, Borates	used as both a herbicide and insecticide
	Sulfur	used as a herbicide, insecticide and fungicide
	Mercury, Lead, Arsenates	metal compounds used for weed, insect and disease control
Petroleum Oils	Horticulture Oil, Dormant Oil, Citrus Oil	Oils are used for insect control, but also as a carrier for some herbicides.
Botanicals	Pyrethrum Rotenone Sabadilla Azadirachtin	Many people consider these natural products but they have not been fully tested. Many of these products are allergic, have high toxicity and may be suspected carcinogens.
Microbial Toxins	Chitin Avermectin-B	Organisms produce molecules that are toxic. Any toxin produced by a bacteria, fungi or other organism.
Biological Agents	*Bacillus thuringiensis* *Bacillus popilliae* *Beauveria spp.* Pathogenic nematodes Lady beetles Lacewings Wasps	These organisms are receiving considerable attention and research efforts for use on turf.
Synthetics	See Appendix	

TABLE 3.

Turfgrass Pesticides Shown to Have Enhanced Degradation

Pesticide	Common Name	Reference
Fungicide	iprodione	Entwistle, A.R. 1983. Phytopathology 73:800.
	benomyl	Woodcock, D. 1978. in Pesticide Microbiology. Academic Press.
	metalaxyl	Bailey, A.M. and M.D. Coffey. 1986. Canadian Journal of Microbiology 32:562-569.
Insecticide	bendiocarb	Tollefson, J.J. 1984. Abstr. American Chemist Society Pesticide Chemistry
	malathion	Matsumura, F. and G.M. Boush. 1966. Science 153:1278-1280.
	diazinon	Sethunathan, B., T.K. Adkya and K. Raghu. 1972. Journal of Agricultural Food Chemistry 20:586-589.
	isophenophos	Niemczyk, H.D. and R.A. Chapman. 1987. Journal Economic Entomology 80:880-882.
Herbicide	2,4-D	Newman, A.S., J.R. Thomas and R.L.Walker. 1952. Proc. Soil Sci. Soc. Am. 14:160-164.
	endothal	Horowitz, B. 1966. Weed Res. 6:168-171.

TABLE 4.

Propagation Methods of Various Turfgrass Species

Common Name	Genus Species	Seed		Vegetatively	Interspecific Hybrid
		Synthetic	Apomictic		
Bermudagrass	Cynodon dactylon	X		X	
	C. dactylon X C. transvaalensis			X	X
St. Augustinegrass	Stenotaphrum secundatum	X			
Centipedegrass	Eremochloa ophiuriodes			X	
Japanese Lawngrass	Zoysia japanica	X		X	
	Z. Japanica X Z. tenufolia			X	X
Mannilagrass	Z. Matrella			X	
Kentucky Bluegrass	Poa pratensis		X		
Perennial Ryegrass	Lolium perenne	X			
Annual Ryegrass	L. multifolium	X			
Tall Fescue	Festuca arundinacea	X			
Hard Fescue	F. longifolia	X			
Red Fescue	F. rubra ssp. rubra	X			
Chewings Fescue	F. rubra ssp. commutata	X		X	
Creeping Bentgrass	Agrostis palustris	X			
Colonial Bentgrass	A. tenuis	X			

TABLE 5.

**APPENDIX
A**

Common Turfgrass Species and Their Botanical Names

COMMON NAME	BOTANICAL NAME
Cool-Season Turfgrasses	
Annual bluegrass	*Poa annua*
Annual ryegrass	*Lolium multiflorum*
Canada bluegrass	*Poa compressa*
Chewings fescue	*Festuca rubra* spp. *rubra*
Colonial bentgrass	*Agrostis tenuis*
Creeping bentgrass	*Agrostis palustris*
Creeping red fescue	*Festuca rubra* spp. *rubra*
Hard fescue	*Festuca ovina* spp. *duriuscula*
Kentucky bluegrass	*Poa pratensis*
Perennial ryegrass	*Lolium perenne*
Rough bluegrass	*Poa trivialis*
Sheep fescue	*Festuca ovina* spp. *ovina*
Tall fescue	*Festuca arundinacea*
Velvet bentgrass	*Agrostis canina*
Warm-Season Turfgrasses	
Bahiagrass	*Paspalum notatum*
Bermudagrass	*Cynodon dactylon*
Blue grama	*Bouteloua gracilis*
Buffalograss	*Buchloe dactyloides*
Carpetgrass	*Axonopus affinis*
Centipedegrass	*Eremochloa ophiuroides*

Kikuyugrass	*Pennisetum clandestinum*
Seashore paspalum	*Paspalum vaginatum*
St. Augustinegrass	*Stenotaphrum secundatum*

Zoysiagrass

Japanese lawngrass	*Zoysia japonica*
Mascarenegrass	*Zoysia tenuifolia*

Some Common Weeds of Turfgrasses

COMMON NAME	BOTANICAL NAME
Grassy weeds	
Annual bluegrass	*Poa annua*
Barnyardgrass	*Echinochloa crusgalli*
Crabgrass	*Digitaria sanguinalis*
Dallisgrass	*Paspalum dilatatum*
Goosegrass	*Eleusine indica*
Green Foxtail	*Setaria viridis*
Nimblewill	*Muchlenbergia schreberi*
Orchardgrass	*Dactylis glomerata*
Quackgrass	*Agropyron repens*
Timothy	*Phleum pratense*
Sandbur	*Cenchrus pauciflorus*
Yellow Foxtail	*Setaria glauca*
Broadleaf weeds	
Bittercress	*Cardamine spp.*
Black medic	*Medicago lupulina*
Broadleaf plantain	*Plantago major*
Buckhorn plantain	*Plantago lanceolata*
Buttercup	*Rananculus spp.*
Chicory	*Cichorium intybus*
Catsear	*Hypochaeris radicata*
Common chickweed	*Stellaria media*
Curly dock	*Rumex crispus*
Dandelion	*Taraxacum officinale*
Ground ivy	*Glechoma hederacea*

Henbit	*Lamium amplexicaule*
Knotweed	*Polygonum aviculare*
Lawn burweed	*Soliva pterosperma*
Mouseear chickweed	*Cerastium vulgatum*
Purslane	*Portulaca oleracea*
Speedwell	*Veronica spp.*
Spurge	*Euphorbia maculata*
White clover	*Trifolium repens*
Yellow woodsorrel	*Oxalis stricta*

APPENDIX C

Common Turfgrass Diseases and Their Associated Pathogens

DISEASE	PATHOGEN
Anthracnose	*Colletotrichum graminicola*
Brown patch	*Rhizoctonia solani, R. zeae*
Copper spot	*Gloeocercospora sorghi*
Dollar spot	*Sclerotinia homoeocarpa*, organism may be more correctly identified as belonging to *Lanzia* and *Moellerodiscus*
Fairy ring	Several species with most prominant being *Marasmius oreades*
Gray leaf spot	*Pyricularia grisea*
Gray snow mold	Several species of *Typhula* including *T. incarnata* and *T. ishikariensis*
Leaf spot, blights	May be caused by different fungi depending on the grass species. Pathogens include *Drechslera* spp., *Cochliobolus* spp., *Curvalaria* spp., *Pyrenophora* spp.
Low temperature basidiomycete	*Coprinus psychromorbidus* (probable cause)
Necrotic ring spot	*Leptosphaeria korrae*
Pink patch	*Limonomyces roseipellis*
Pink snow mold	*Microdochium nivale* (formally: Fusarium nivale)
Powdery mildew	*Erysiphe graminis*
Pythium blight	*Pythium* spp. including species such as *P. ultimum, P. graminicola, P. aphanidermatum*
Red thread	*Laetisaria fuciformis*
Rusts	
Bermudagrass rust	*Puccinia cynodontis*

159

Crown rust	*Puccinia coronata*
Leaf rust	*Puccinia recondita*
Stem rust	*Puccinia graminis*
St. Augustinegrass rust	*Puccinia stenotaphri*
Zoysiagrass rust	*Puccinia zoysiae*
Slime molds	*Plasmodium*
Southern blight	*Sclerotium rolfsii*
Spring dead spot	*Leptosphaeria korrae, L. narmari*
Summer patch	*Magnaporthe poae*
Smut, flag	*Urocystis agropyri*
Smut, stripe	*Ustilago striiformis*
Take-all patch	*Gaeumannomyces graminis*
Yellow tuft	*Scherophthora macrospora*

APPENDIX
D

Common Insect Pests of Turfgrasses

COMMON NAME	SCIENTIFIC NAME
Soil Inhabitants	
Black turfgrass atenius	*Ataenius spretulus*
Bluegrass billbugs	*Sphenophorus* spp.
Ground pearls	*Margarodes meridionalis*
Mole crickets	*Scapteriscus acletus*
Grubs	
Japanese beetles	*Popillia japonica*
June beetles	*Phyllophaga* spp.
Northern masked chafers	*Cyclocephala borealis*
Southern masked chafers	*Cyclocephala immaculata*
Thatch Inhabitants	
Black cutworms	*Agrotis ipsilon*
Bronzed cutworms	*Nephelodes minians*
Fall armyworms	*Spodoptera frugiperda*
Hairy chinchbugs	*Blissus leucopterus*
Hyperodes weevils	*Hyperodes* spp.
Sod webworms	*Crambus* spp.
Southern chinchbugs	*Blissus insularis*
Stem and Leaf Inhabitants	
Bermudagrass mites	*Eriophyes cynodoniensis*
Bermudagrass scales	*Odonaspis ruthae*
Clover mites	*Bryobia praetiosa*
Rhodesgrass scales	*Antonina graminis*
Winter grain mites	*Penthaleus major*

APPENDIX
E

Commonly Used Fungicides for Disease Control in Turf

COMMON NAME	TRADE NAMES	COMMENTS
Chemical Family: Mercury		
Mercury compounds	Calo Clor, Calo Gran PMA (phenyl mercuric acetate)	The mercury fungicides were one of the first fungicides used on turf. Mercury has broad-spectrum activity and acts as an erradicant which is highly toxic to fungi. Currently mercuries are confined to use on snow mold diseases since they have been found to accumulate in fish and mammals, and are highly persistent in the environment.
Chemical Family: Dithiocarbamates		
Maneb	Dithane FZ, Dithane M-22,	These kinds of products have broad-spectrum control properties and are used as protectants.
Zineb	Dithane Z-78, Zineb	
Mancozeb	Fore, Formec, LESCO 4, Dithane M-45	
Thiram	Spotrete, Thiramid	
Chemical Family: Dicarboximides		
Iprodione	Chipco 26019, Proturf Fungicide VI	These fungicides were developed in the mid-1970s and are systemic in nature. Research has shown that these fungicides are both acro-
Vinclozolin	Vorlan (Curalan & Touche)	

162

these fungicides are both acropetally and symplatically. These fungicides are considered to have a broad spectrum of control.

Chemical Family:
Benzimidazoles

Benomyl	Tersan 1991, Rockland, Lebanon Fungicide Type B	Benomyl became available in the late 1960s. These fungicides are characterized by acropetal transport and broad-spectrum control, and were the first site specific fungicides with reported fungal resistance.
Thiophanate-methyl	Cleary's 3336, Fungo 50	

Chemical Family:
Sterol Inhibitors

Fenarimol	Rubigan	This group of fungicides is the newest chemistry developed.
Triademifon	Bayleton	These fungicides are systemic and work by interfering with sterol biosynthesis. This group has a broad-spectrum range of control.
Propiconazole	Banner	

Pythium Controlling Fungicides (from different chemical families):

Metalaxyl	Subdue, Proturf Pythium Control	Characteristic of these compounds is their narrow spectrum. Few, if any diseases, besides the pythium fungi or closely related fungi of the order Peronosporales (water molds like yellow tuft). The early pythium fungicides were Tersan SP and Koban. These fungicides were effective for only a few short days. In the early 1980s the systemic pythium fungicides Subdue and Banol became available providing up to 4 weeks control (2 to 3
Propamocarb	Banol	
Fosetyl Aluminum	Aliette	
Chloroneb	Tersan SP, Teremec Sp, Proturf Fungicide II	
Etridiazol	Koban	

weeks more reliable). The most recent pythium fungicide, Aliette, is an interesting compound since it does not initially appear to have fungicidal activity, but conveys greater host resistance.

Additional Fungicides (in different chemical families):

Anilazine	Dyrene, Lescorene, Proturf Fungicide II, Lofts Lawn Fungicide	Listed to the left are important fungicides currently available that generally provide broad-spectrum control. Since these compounds represent different chemical groups they are bunched together here.
Chlorothalonil	Daconil 2787, Lebanon Type Fungicide D	They are protectant type fungicides that do not have systemic activity (however PCNB may be locally systemic).
PCNB (pentachloronitrobenzine)	Terraclor, Turfcide, Scotts FFII, LESCO PCNB	

APPENDIX
F

Commonly Used Insecticides for Insect Control in Turf

CHEMICAL FAMILY	COMMON NAME	TRADE NAME	MODE OF ACTION	COMMENTS
Organo-phosphates	Diazinon	Diazinon	cholinisterase inhibitor	Diazinon has been banned for use on sod fields and golf courses.
	Chlorpyrifos	Dursban	cholinisterase inhibitor	
	Trichlorfon	Dylox, Proxol	cholinisterase inhibitor	
	Ethoprop	Mocap	cholinisterase inhibitor	
	Isophenphos	Oftanol	cholinisterase inhibitor	
	Acephate	Orthene Turf	cholinisterase inhibitor	
	Isazofos	Triumph	cholinisterase inhibitor	
Carbamates	Bendiocarb	Ficam, Turcam	cholinisterase inhibitor	Similar in action to organophosphates.
	Carbaryl	Sevin	cholinisterase inhibitor	
Pyrethroids	Fluvalinate	Maverick	nervous system	Extracted from certain flowers including the chrysanthemum.

APPENDIX
G

Commonly Used Herbicides For Weed Control in Turf

CHEMICAL FAMILY	COMMON NAME	TRADE NAME	MODE OF ACTION	COMMENTS
Acetamides	Metolachlor	Pennant	meristematic inhibitor	Used on some warm-season turfs such as bermudagrass for preemergent weed control.
Amides	Diphenamid	Enide	meristematic inhibitor	These herbicides are primarily used for annual grass control in some warm-season turfs.
	Pronomide	Kerb	meristematic inhibitor	
	Napropamide	Devrinol	meristematic inhibitor	
Benzoics	Dicamba	Banvel	plant hormone-like	Used postemergently for broadleaf weed control.
Benzothia-diazole	Bentazon	Basagran	photosynthetic inhibitor	Used to control nutsedge. Thorough coverage provides most effective results.
Dinitroanilines (DNAs)	Benefin	Balan	meristematic inhibitor	DNAs are used for preemergent annual grass weed control. Some of the dinitroan-ilines can give early post and some control of broadleaf weeds. This group of herbi-cides are the most widely used in lawn
	Pendimethalin	Scotts LESCO	meristematic inhibitor	
	Trifluralin +			
	Benefin	Team	meristematic inhibitor	
	Oryzalin +			

166

	Benefin	XL	meristematic inhibitor	care for annual grass control.
	Prodiamine	Barricade	meristematic inhibitor	New compound.
Imidazolinones	Imazaquin	Image	meristematic inhibitor	Used on warm-season turfgrasses, such as bermudagrass, as a preemergent.
OrganicArsen-icals	DSMA	***	contact	DSMA and MSMA provide postemergent annual grass control. Cacodilic acid is non-selective.
	MSMA	***	contact	
	Cacodylic acid	Phytar	contact	
Oxyphenoxy propanoic acids	Fenoxyprop-ethyl	Acclaim	meristematic inhibitor	Acclaim is used for postemergent control of crabgrass. Poast is used in warm-season turfs.
	Sethoxydim	Poast	meristematic inhibitor	
Pyridine carboxylic acid	Triclopyr	Turflon	plant hormone-like	Effective on perennial broadleaf weeds as a postemergent applica-tion.
	Triclopyr + Clopyralid	Confront	plant hormone-like	
Phenoxy acids	2,4-D	***	plant hormone-like	Phenoxies are used for postemergent broadleaf weed con-trol. Most widely used herbicides in the lawn care business. MCPP controls clover.
	Dicloprop		plant hormone-like	
	MCPA		plant hormone-like	
	Mecoprop (MCPP)		plant hormone-like	
Phosophono Amino Acids	Glyphosate	Roundup	meristematic inhibitor	Non-selective control.
Sulfonylureas	Chlosulfuron	LESCO	meristematic	A spot treatment for the

167

		TFC	inhibitor	removal of tall fescue from Kentucky bluegrass.
Phenylureas	Siduron	Tupersan	photosynthetic inhibitor	Preemergent weed control especially for use on new seedling turf.
Triazines	Atrazine	AAtrex	photosynthetic inhibitor	Used on warm-season turfs.
	Metribuzin	Sencor	photosynthetic inhibitor	
	Simazine	Princep	photosynthetic inhibitor	

Others (herbicides without specific chemical family):

	Bensulide	Betasan	not fully understood	Preemergent weed control. Inhibits root growth.
	DCPA	Dacthal	not fully understood; kills germinating seeds	Preemergent weed control. Does show postemergent control of speedwell.
	Oxidiazon	Ronstar	pigment inhibitor	Preemergent weed control in cool- and warm-season grasses.
	Endothal	Endothal	contact	Used for annual bluegrass control.
	Ethofumasate	Prograss	not fully understood	Used as both a pre- and postemergent. Primarily used on warm-season grasses, but

			is used for annual bluegrass control in Kentucky bluegrass, ryegrass and bent-grass.
Isoxaben	Gallery	not fully understood	Unique broadleaf weed control since it is a preemergent.
dithiopyr	Dimen-sion	meristematic inhibitor	Used for preemergent annual grass control. Will also control annual grasses early post.

*** number of trade names   (Danneberger, 1991)

References

CHAPTER 1

Neiburger, J., J.G. Edinger and W.D. Bonner. 1982. Understanding Our Atmospheric Environment. W.H. Freeman & Co., Calif.

Strahler, A.H. and A.H. Strahler. 1984. Elements of Physical Geography. John Wiley & Sons. N.Y.

Trewartha, G.T. and Horn. 1980. An Introduction to Climate. McGraw-Hill Co., N.Y

CHAPTER 2

Barrios, E.P., F.J. Sundstrom, D. Babcock and L. Leger. 1986. Agronomy Journal 78:270-273.

Brede, A.D. and J.M. Duich. 1986. Agronomy Journal 78:179-184.

Biran, I. and I. Bushkin-Harav. 1981. HortScience 16:74-76.

Burton, G.W., J.E. Hook, J.L. Butler and R.E. Hellwig. 1988. Agronomy Journal 80:557-560.

DiPaolo, J.M. 1990. *Grounds Maintenance* 25(6):24-32.

McCarty, L.B., D.W. Roberts, L.C. Miller and J.A. Brittain. 1990. Journal of Agronomic Education 19:155-159.

McDonald, M.B., L. Copeland, D. Grabe and A. Knapp. 1992. *in* Cool-Season Grasses Monograph. Madison, Wis. (in review).

McBee, G.G. 1969. Crop Science 9:14-17.

Mehall, B.J., R.J. Hull and C.R. Skogley. 1984. Agronomy Journal 76:47-50.

Powell, J.B., G.W. Burton and J.R. Young. 1974. Crop Science 14:327-330.

Starr, C., and R. Taggart. 1989. Biology: The Unity & Diversity of Life. Wadsworth Publishing Co., Calif.

Watschke, T.L., R.E. Schmidt, E.W. Carson and R.E. Blaser. 1972. Crop Science 12:87-90.

CHAPTER 3

Bell, M.K. 1974. *in* Biology of Plant Litter Decomposition. ed. C.H. Dickinson and G.J.F. Pugh. Academic Press. London.

Bennett, J.P. and V.C. Runeckles. 1977. Crop Science 17:443-445.

Bowman, D.C., J.L. Paul and W.B. Davis. 1987. HortScience 22:84-87.

Bowman, D.C., J.L. Paul, W.B. Davis and S.H. Nelson. 1989. Journal of American Society of Horticulture Science 114:229-233.

Brennan E. and P.M. Halisky. 1970. Phytopathology 60:1544-1546.

Brown, K.W., J.C. Thomas and R.L. Duble. 1982. Agronomy Journal 74:947-950.

Dernoeden, P.H., J.N. Crahay and D.B. Davis. 1991. Crop Science 31:1674-1680.

Geron, C.A., T.K. Danneberger, S.J. Traina, T.J. Logan and J.R. Street. Journal Environmental Quality. 22:119-125.

Hummel, N.W. 1989. Agronomy Journal 81:290-294.

Hummel, N.W. and D.V. Waddington. 1986. HortScience 21:1155-1156.

Johnston, W.J., R.L. Haaland and R. Dickens. 1983. Crop Science 23:235-236.

Joo, Y.K., N.K. Christians and J.M. Bremner. 1987. Journal of Fertilizer Issues 3:98-102.

Joo, Y.K., N.K. Christians and J.M. Bremner. 1991. HortScience 26:537-539.

Ledeboer, F.B. and C.R. Skogley. 1967. Agronomy Journal 59:320-322.

Mancino, C.F., W.A. Torello and D.J. Wehner. 1988. Agronomy Journal 80:148-153.

O'Neil, K.J. and R.N. Carrow. 1983. Agronomy Journal 75:177-180.

Richards, G.A., C.L. Mulchi and J.R. Hall. 1980. Journal Environmental Quality 9:49-53.

Sionit, N., H. Hellmers and B.R. Strain. 1982. Agronomy Journal 74:721-725.

Titko, S., J.R. Street and T.J. Logan. 1987. Agronomy Journal 79:535-540.

Torello, W.A. and D.J. Wehner. 1983. Agronomy Journal 75:654-656.

Wesely, R.W., R.C. Sherman, E.J. Kinbacher and S.R. Lowry. 1987. HortScience 22:1278-1280.

CHAPTER 4

Anonymous, 1990. U.S. EPA National Pesticide Survey Phase I Report (Ex. Summary) 10 p.

Beard, J.B. and D.P. Martin. 1970. Agronomy Journal 62:257-259.

Beard, J.B. 1973. Turfgrass: Science and Culture, Prentice-Hall Englewood Cliffs, N.J.

Beard, J.B. 1986. *Grounds Maintenance* 21(1):60-62.

Casnoff, D.M., R.L. Green and J.B. Beard. 1989. *in* Proc. 6th International Turfgrass Res. Conf. 129-131.

Cohen, S.Z. 1990. *Golf Course Management* 58(2):26-44.

Endo, R.M. 1967. California Turf Culture 17:12-13.

Fry, J.D. and J.D. Butler. 1989. HortScience 24:73-75.

Green, R.L., J.B. Beard and D.M. Casnoff. 1990. HortScience 27:760-761.

Green, R.L., S.I. Sifers, C.E. Atkins and J.B. Beard. 1991. HortScience 26:264-266.

Hammer, M.J. 1986. *in* Water and Wastewater Technology. John Wiley, New York.

Harivandi, A. 1988. *Golf Course Management* 56(1):106,107,189-193.

Johnson, S.J. and N.E. Christians. 1985. HortScience 20:772-773.

Kim, K.S. and J.B. Beard. 1988. Crop Science 28:328-331.

Kopec, D.M., R.C. Shearman and T.P. Riordan. 1988. HortScience 23:300-301.

Shearman, R.C. 1986. HortScience 21:455-457.

Watschke, T.L. 1990. *Golf Course Management* 58(2):18-24.

CHAPTER 5

Beard, J.B. 1966. Michigan Quarterly Bulletin 48(3):377-383.

Blum, A. 1988. Plant Breeding for Stress Environments. CRC Press, Boca Raton, Fla.

Branham, B.E. and T.K. Danneberger. 1989. Agronomy Journal 81:749-752.

Burke, M.J., L.V. Gusta, H.A. Quamme, C.J. Wieser and P.H. Li. 1976. Annual Review of Plant Physiology 27:507-528.

DiPaola, J.M. 1984. Agronomy Journal 76:951-953.

Duff, D.T. and J.B. Beard. 1966. Agronomy Journal 58:495-497.

Goss, R.L. and A.G. Law. 1967. Agronomy Journal 59:516-518.

Gusta, L.V., J.D. Butler, C. Rajashekar and M.J. Burke. 1980. HortScience 15:494-496.

Karnok, K.J. and J.B. Beard. 1983. HortScience 18:95-97.

Mehall, B.J., R.J. Hull and C.R. Skogley. 1984. Agronomy Journal 76:47-50.

Moon, J.W., D.M. Kopec, E. Fallahi, C.F. Mancino, D.C. Slack and K. Jordan. 1990. Journal of American Society for Horticultural Science 115:478-481.

Rajashekar, C., D. Tao and P.H. Li. 1983. HortScience 18:91-93.

Sherman, R.C. 1989. *Golf Course Management* 57(2):23-30.

Shetlar, D. 1991. *Lawn & Landscape Maintenance* 12(4):68-72.

Vegis, A. 1964. Annual Review of Plant Physiology 15:185-224.

Wehner, D.J. and T.L. Watschke. 1981. Agronomy Journal 73:79-84.

White, D.B. and M.H. Smithberg. 1980. V International Turfgrass Conference 5:149-154.

White, R.H. and R.E. Schmidt. 1989. Crop Science 29:768-773.

White, R.H. and R.E. Schmidt. 1990. Journal of American Society for Horticultural Science 115:57-61.

CHAPTER 6

Baker, S.W. 1981. Journal Sports Turf Research Institute 57:9-23.

Baker, S.W. 1988. Journal Sports Turf Research Institute 64:133-141.

Beard, J.B. 1973. Turfgrass: Science and Culture. Prentice-Hall, N.J.

Beard, J.B. 1982. Turf Management for Golf Courses. MacMillan Publishing Co., N.Y.

Canaway, P.M. 1978. Journal Sports Turf Research Institute 54:7-14.

Canaway, P.M. 1981. Journal Sports Turf Research Institute 57:108-121.

Canaway, P.M. 1983. Journal Sports Turf Research Institute 59:107-123.

Carrow, R.N. 1980. Agronomy Journal 72:1038-1042.

Cole, M.A. and A.J. Turgeon. 1978. Soil Biology and Biochemistry 10:181-186.

Gould, C.J. 1973. Golf Course Superintendent 41(3):44-46.

Hudson, R.A. 1992. Ph.D. thesis. The Ohio State University.

Hurto, K.A., A.J. Turgeon and L.A. Spomer. 1980. Agronomy Journal 72:165-167.

James, S.W. 1991. Ecology 72:2101-2109.

Ledeboer, F.B. and C.R. Skogley. 1967. Agronomy Journal 59:320-322.

McCoy, E.L. 1991. Agronomy Journal 84:375-381.

Meinhold, J.H., R.L. Duble, R.W. Weaver and E.C. Holt. 1973. Agronomy Journal 65:833-835.

Murphy, J.A. and P.E. Rieke. 1991. *Golf Course Management* 59(7):6,7,10,12,14,20,22.

Murphy, J.A., P.E. Rieke and A.E. Erickson. 1993. Agronomy Journal, 85:1-9.

Nelson, K.E., A.J. Turgeon and J.R. Street. 1980. Agronomy Journal 72:487-492.

Potter, D.A., B.L. Bridges and F.C. Gordon. 1985. Agronomy Journal 77:367-372.

Randell, R.J., J.D. Butler and T.D. Hughes. 1972. HortScience 7:64-65.

Sartain, J.B. and B.G. Volk. 1984. Agronomy Journal 76:359-362.

Shearman, R.C., B.E. Anderson, D.M. Kopec and T.P. Riordan. 1986. HortScience 21:1164.

Shearman, R.C. and J.B. Beard. 1975a. Agronomy Journal 67:208-211.

Shearman, R.C. and J.B. Beard. 1975b. Agronomy Journal 67:215-218.

Shearman, R.C., A.H. Bruneau, E.J. Kinbacher and T.P. Riordan. 1983. HortScience 18:97-99.

Shearman, R.C. and J.E. Watkins. 1985. HortScience 20:388-390.

Shildrick, J.P. 1985. Journal Sports Turf Research Institute 61:8-25.

Sills, M.J. and R.N. Carrow. 1983. Agronomy Journal 75:488-492.

Smiley, R.W. and M.M. Craven. 1979. Soil Biology Biochemistry 11:349-353.

Smiley, R.W., M.C. Fowler, R.T. Kane, A.M. Petrovic and R.A. White. 1985. Agronomy Journal 77:597-602.

Syers, J.K., A.N. Sharpley and D.R. Keeney. 1979. Soil Biology and Biochemistry 11:181-185.

Swift, M.J., O.W. Heal and J.M. Anderson. 1979. Decomposition in Terrestrial Ecosystems. Blackwell Scientific. Oxford.

Taylor, D.H. and G.R. Blake. 1979. Soil Science Society of America Journal 43:394-398.

Taylor, D.H. and G.R. Blake. 1982. Soil Science Society of America Journal 46:616-619.

Taylor, D.H. and G.R. Blake. 1984. Agronomy Journal 76:583-587.

Turgeon, A.J., R.P. Freeborg and W.N. Bruce. 1975. Agronomy Journal 67:563-565.

Waddington, D.V. 1969. *in* Turfgrass Science. American Society of Agronomy Monographs. Madison, Wis.

CHAPTER 7

Danneberger, T.K., J.M. Vargas Jr. and A.L. Jones. 1984. Phytopathology 74:448-451.

Danneberger, T.K., J.M. Vargas Jr., P.E. Rieke and J.R. Street. 1983. Agronomy Journal 75:35-38.

Dernoeden, P.H., J.N. Crahay and D.B. Davis. 1991. Crop Science 31:1674-1680.

Donald, C.M. 1963. Advances in Agronomy 15:1-118.

Hutchinson, G.E. 1957. Cold Springs Harbor Symposium on Quantitative Biology 22:415-427.

Hall, T.J., P.O. Larsen and A.F. Schmitthenner. 1980. Plant Disease 64:1100-1103.

Miller, S.A., G.D. Grothaus, F.P. Peterson, J.H. Rittenburg, K.A. Plumley and R.K. Lankow. 1990. *in* Integrated Pest Management for Turfgrass and Ornamental. Editors Leslie, A.R. and R.L. Metcalf. Lawrence, Kansas.

Smiley, R.W., P.H. Dernoeden and B.B. Clark. 1992. Compendium of Turfgrass Diseases. American Phytopathological Society.

Smith, J.D., N. Jackson and A.R. Woolhouse. 1989. Fungal Diseases of Amenity Turfgrasses. E and F.N. Spon. New York, N.Y.

Tillman, D. and D. Wedin. 1991. Nature 353:653-655.

Vargas Jr., J.M. 1981. Management of Turfgrass Diseases. Burgess Publishing Co., MN.

CHAPTER 8

Ballare, C.L., A.L. Scopel and R.A. Sanchez. 1990. Science 247:329-332.

Ballare, C.L., A.L. Scopel, R.A. Sanchez and S.R. Radosevich. 1992. Photochemistry and Photobiology 56:777-788.

Begon, M., J.L. Harper and C.R. Townsend. 1990. Ecology: individuals, populations and communities. Blackwell Scientific Publication, Cambridge, Mass.

Burdon, J.J. and G.A. Chivers. 1982. Annual Review of Phytopathology 20:143-166.

Canaway, P.M. and J.W. Hacker. 1988. Journal of Sports Turf Research 64:53-74.

Clay, K. 1990. Oecologia 73:358-362.

Couch, H.B. and B.D. Smith. 1991. Crop Protection 10:386-390.

Danneberger, T.K., M.B. McDonald, C.A. Geron and P. Kumari. 1992. HortScience 27:28-30.

Dekker, J. 1976. Annual Review of Plant Pathology 14:405-428.

Dekker, J. 1985. Pesticide Biochemistry and Toxicology 4:165-218.

Dudeck, A.E. and C.H. Peacock. 1986. Crop Science 26:177-179.

Flemming, R.A. 1981. Phytopathology 71:8-12.

Forgash, A.J. 1984. Pesticide Biochemistry and Physiology 22:178-186.

Hathcock, A.L., P.H. Dernoeden, T.R. Turner and M.S. McIntosh. 1984. Agronomy Journal 76:879-883.

Hutchinson, G.E. 1957. Cold Springs Harbor Symposium on Quantitative Biology 22:415-427.

Kable, P.F. and H. Jeffery. 1980. Phytopathology 80:8-12.

Koller, W. and H. Scheinpflug. 1987. Plant Disease 71:1066-1074.

Lonsdale, W.M. and A.R. Watkinson. 1982. New Phytologist 90:431-435.

Lonsdale, W.M. 1990. Ecology 71:1373-1388.

Lush, W.M. 1987. Australian Journal Experiment Agriculture 27:323-327.

Lush, W.M. 1990. Agronomy Journal 82:505-511.

Lush, W.M. and P.R. Franz. 1991. Agronomy Journal 83:800-803.

Lush, W.M. and M.E. Rodgers. 1992. Journal of Applied Ecology 29:611-618.

McKenzie, J.A. and M.J. Whitten. 1984. Australian Journal of Biological Science 37:45-52.

Rice, J.S., B.W. Pinkerton, W.C. Stringer and D.J. Undersander. 1990. Crop Science 30:1303-1306.

Sanders, P.L. 1983. Phytopathology 73:375.

Sanders, P.L., E.P. Gilbride and H. Cole. 1982. Phytopathology 72:261.

Sanders, P.L., W.J. Houser, P.J. Parish and H.Cole Jr. 1985. Plant Disease 69:939-943.

Skylakakis, G. 1983. Annual Review of Phytopathology 21:117-135.

Vargas Jr., J.M., R. Golembiewski and A.R. Detweiler. 1992. *Golf Course Management* 60(3):50,52,54.

White, J. 1980. *in* Demography and Evolution in Plant Populations. University of California Press, Berkeley.

CHAPTER 9

Beard, J.B., P.E. Rieke, A.J. Turgeon and J.M. Vargas Jr. 1978. Michigan State Agricultural Experiment Station Report 352.

Bennett, O.L. and B.D. Doss. 1960. Agronomy Journal 52:204-207.

Bergelson, J. 1990. Ecology 71:2157-2165.

Bingham, S.W., R.E. Schmidt and C.K. Curry. 1969. Agronomy Journal 61:908-911.

Brede, A.D. and J.M. Duich. 1984. Agronomy Journal 76:875-879.

Brede, A.D. and J.M. Duich. 1986. Agronomy Journal 78:179-184.

Danneberger, T.K. 1990. *Lawn & Landscape Maintenance* 11(12):30-31.

Doss, B.D., D.A. Ashley and O.L. Bennett. 1960. Agronomy Journal 52:569-572.

Dudeck, A.E. and C.H. Peacock. 1986. Journal American Society for Horticultural Science 111:844-848.

Eggens, J. and Wright. 1985. HortScience 20:109-110.

Glinski, D.S., H.A. Mills, K.J. Karnok and R.N. Carrow. 1989. HortScience 25:932-933.

Grime, J.P. and R. Hunt. 1975. Journal of Ecology 63:393-422.

Hays, K.L., J.F. Barber, M.P. Kenna and T.G. McCollum. 1991. HortScience 26:180-182.

Johnson, B.J. 1975. Weed Science 23:110-115.

Johnson, B.J. 1986. Agronomy Journal 78:495-498.

Johnson, B.J. 1987. Agriculture Experiment Station Report 358. Univ. of Georgia.

Johnson, B.J. 1988. Journal of American Society for Horticultural Science 113:662-666.

Juska, F.V. and A.A. Hanson. 1969. Agronomy Journal 61:466-468.

King, J. 1971. Journal of British Grassland Society 26:221-229.

Krans, J.V. 1983. Agriculture Experiment Station Report 8: No. 5. Mississippi State University.

Law, R., A.D. Bradshaw and P.D. Putwain. 1977. Evolution 31:233-246.

Law, R. 1981. Ecology 62:1267-1277.

Lush, W.M. 1988a. Journal of Applied Ecology 25:977-988.

Lush, W.M. 1988b. Journal of Applied Ecology 25:989-997.

Lush, W.M. 1989. Weed Science 37:54-59.

Mazur, A.R. and D.F. Wagner. 1987. HortScience 22:1276-1278.

Mazur, A.R. 1988. Journal of American Society for Horticultural Science 113:367-373.

McDonald, M.B., L. Copeland, A. Knapp and D. Grabe. *in* Cool- Season Grasses Monograph. Madison,WI (in review).

Solbrig, O.T. and B.B. Simpson. 1974. Journal of Ecology 62:473-486.

Solbrig, O.T. and B.B. Simpson. 1977. Journal of Ecology 65:427-430.

Southwood, T.R.E. 1977. Journal of Animal Ecology 46:337-365.

Standifer, L.C. and P.W. Wilson. 1988. Weed Research 28:359-363.

Stevens, O.A. 1932. American Journal of Botany 19:784-794.

Tilman, D. 1986. *in* Plant Ecology. E.J. Crawley, Ed. Blackwell Scientific Publishing.

Waddington, D.V., T.R. Turner, J.M. Duich and E.L.Moberg. 1978. Agronomy Journal 70:713-718.

Wehner, D.J. and T.L. Watschke. 1981. Agronomy Journal 73:79-84.

Youngner, V.G. 1959. Journal of the British Grassland Society 14:233-247.

CHAPTER 10

Arnold, T.B. and D.A. Potter. 1987. Environmental Entomology 16:100-105.

Brede, A.D. and J.L. Brede. 1988. Agronomy Journal 80:27-30.

Cockfield, S.D. and D.A. Potter. 1983. Environmental Entomology 12:1260-1264.

Cockfield, S.D. and D.A. Potter. 198 Journal Economic Entomology 77:1542-1544.

Cockfield, S.D. and D.A. Potter. 1987. Canadian Entomology 117:423-429.

Danneberger, T.K. 1991. *Lawn & Landscape Maintenance* 12(3):72-78.

Dernoeden, P.H. 1989. HortScience 25:796-798.

Dernoeden, P.H. and J.M. Krouse. 1990. Fungicide and Nematicide Tests 45:286.

Dernoeden, P.H., J.J. Murray and N.R. O'Neill. 1985. *in* Proceedings 5th International Turfgrass Research Conference, Avignon, France.

Flint, M.L. and R.V.D. Bosch. 1981. *in* Introduction to Integrated Pest Management. Plenum Press, New York. 240 p.

Flor, H.H. 1971. Annual Review of Phytopathology 9:275-296.

Freeman, S. and R.J. Rodriguez. 1993. Science 260:75-78.

Goatley, J.M. and R.E. Schmidt. 1990. Agronomy Journal 82:901-905.

Goatley, J.M. and R.E. Schmidt. 1991. HortScience26:254-255.

Grange, A.C. and V.K. Brown. 1989. Oikos 56:351-356.

Greaves, M.P. 1987. *in* Pesticide Effects on Soil Microflora. Taylor and Francis, London.

Haley, J.E., D.J. Wehner, T.W. Fermanian and A.J.Turgeon. 1985. HortScience 20:105-107.

Kane, R.T. and R.W. Smiley. 1983. Agronomy Journal 75:469-473.

Karr, G.W., R.T. Gudauskas and R. Dickens. 1979. Phytopathology 69:279-282.

Madison, J.H. 1962. Agronomy Journal 54:407-412.

Moore, P.D. 1990. Nature 344:492.

Nelson, E.B. 1990. Cornell University Turfgrass Times (CUTT) 1(1):1,4.

Obrigawitch, T., A.R. Martin and F.W. Roeth. 1983. Weed Science 31:187-192.

Osgerby, J.M. 1973. Pesticide Research 4:247-258.

Radko, A.M., R.E. Engel and J.R. Trout. 1981. Green Section Record 19(1):9-13.

Schuster, E. and D. Schroder. 1990. Soil Biology and Biochemistry 22:367-373.

Shetlar, D.J., P.E. Suleman and R. Georgis. 1988. Journal Economic Entomology 81:1318-1322.

Smiley, R.W. 1981. Plant Disease 65:17-23.

Steinegger, D.H., R.C. Sherman, T.P. Riordan and E.J. Kinbacher. 1983. Agronomy Journal 75:479-480.

Sweeney, P.M. and T.K. Danneberger. 1993. *Lawn & Landscape Maintenance* 14(1):58-62.

Turgeon, A.J. and J.M. Vargas Jr. 1980. Proceeding of the 3rd International Turfgrass Conference 3:19-30.

Warren, C.G., P.L. Sanders and H. Cole Jr. 1976. Plant Disease Reporter 60:932-935.

Welton, F.Λ. and J.C. Carroll. 1938. Ohio Agricultural Experiment Station Special Circular 53: 107-115.

Glossary

Acclimation. A period of time when plants become accustomed to a set of given environmental conditions.

Actinomycete. A filamentous (thread-like) bacteria.

Adenosine triphosphate (ATP). A sugar phosphate molecule containing high energy bonds that provide energy for metabolic reactions.

Adiabatic process. A change in the temperature of air because of compression or expansion. Heat neither leaves nor enters the system. In this text, a thunderstorm.

Air Mass. Extensive body of air. A fairly uniform characteristic of temperature and moisture throughout.

Allele. One of two alternate forms of a gene found at a gene locus. In the context of this book, one allele may confer pesticide resistance while another confers pesticide sensitivity.

Amino acid. A molecule having an amino group (NH_2) and an acid group (-COOH) serving as the building blocks for proteins.

Antagonistic. As it applies to living organisms, see suppressive organism. As it applies to pesticides, the combination of two or more chemicals resulting in a loss of control of the targeted organism.

Anticyclone. The center of a high atmospheric pressure area.

Antitranspirant. A substance that inhibits or greatly reduces transpiration from the leaf.

Asexual reproduction. Production of new individuals vegetatively without the union of two gametes (sperm, egg).

Atmosphere. Gases that surround the Earth held by gravity.

Bacteria. A single cell organism that does not contain a nucleus (DNA moves freely in the cell). In turf, bacteria are primarily decomposers but some are pathogens.

Bar. A unit of pressure.

Biomass. Expressed as the dry weight in grams of organic matter per given area, normally meters. It is a measurement of the living component in an ecosystem.

Biosphere. All living organisms of the Earth and the environments in which they interact including portions of the atmosphere, lithosphere and hydrosphere.

Blend. A combination of two or more cultivars of the same turfgrass species.

Boundary layer. A thin layer of air that contains a large amount of water vapor. The boundary layer is a barrier to leaf evaporation.

Calcareous. Containing lime or limestone. Often used to classify soils containing a high amount of calcium.

Carrying capacity (K). The limit to the amount of life that can be supported by a habitat.

Cation exchange capacity. The total amount of exchangeable cations that the soil can absorb. Cation exchange capacity is expressed as milliequivalents per 100 grams of soil.

Chaos. Wide fluctuation in biomass accumulation over time.

Chromosome. A DNA molecule that contains hereditary information that can be passed down from one organism to another.

Climate. Generalized weather conditions for an area based on data gathered for a long period of time.

Community. The populations of all species found in a habitat.

Competitive exclusion. The elimination of one species from a habitat by another through interspecific competition.

Condensation. The changing of water vapor from the gaseous state to a liquid (water) or solid (ice).

Convection (atmosphere). Pertains to strong updrafts of air molecules localized in convection cells. Normally, associated with strong storms such as thunderstorms.

Convection (leaf blade). A means of transferring heat from the leaf blade (leaf cooling process). Warm air absorbing heat from the leaf surface rises and is replaced with cooler air.

Cool-season turfgrass. A turfgrass species with an optimum temperature range for growth of 60 to 75 F. Examples of cool-season turfgrasses include the bluegrasses, ryegrasses, bentgrasses and fescues.

Cyclone. The center of a low atmospheric pressure area.

Detritus. Organic matter particles in varying stages of decomposition.

Dew point. Temperature at which the air is saturated and moisture may form.

Disturbance. An event that creates open spaces in turf which can be colonized by different species. Disturbances are associated with pests and human activity.

Dormancy. A physical or physiological state of suspended or greatly reduced plant growth.

DNA (deoxyribonucleic acid). A double-stranded, helical-coiled molecule where the genetic information of the organism is stored.

Ecology. The science that studies living organisms and how they relate to the environment.

Ecosystem. An identifiable self-contained entity containing plants and animals who associate with each other, and the physical and chemical environments in which the organisms interact.

Effluent water. Water that contains a level of contaminates from sewage.

Equator. The latitude midway between the north and south pole. It is designated as the 0° latitude.

Endophyte. In turf, an organism — primarily the fungus *Acremonium coenophiallum* — which infects the seeds of certain cultivars of perennial ryegrass, tall fescue and fine fescue. Enhanced establishment rate and resistance to surface-feeding insects have been associated with endophyte-infected seed.

Enzymes. Enzymes are specialized proteins that catalyze numerous cellular reactions. Enzymes do not enter the reactions themselves and are not altered or destroyed by the reactions.

Evapotranspiration. The loss of water to the atmosphere from the soil and vegetation.

Fiber. The least decomposed of the soil organic matter.

Fitness. The contribution an individual makes to the gene pool of the next generation in relation to the contribution made by other individuals of the population. Primarily used in this text as a means of characterizing a pesticide resistant population to the pesticide sensitive population.

Freezing. A change from the liquid state (water) to the solid state (ice).

Front. The point of contact between two unlike air masses.

Fungus. A small organism lacking chlorophyll that in most cases is multicellular. Fungi are important as decomposers of organic matter and as pathogens.

Gause hypothesis. If two competing species coexist in a stable environment, it is because they have different realized niches. However, if no differences exist between their realized niches, one of the species will be eliminated.

Gene. A specific region of DNA that is the basic unit of inheritance.

Gibberellic acids. A group of growth promoting substances involved in a number of plant growth responses.

Grass. A member of the family gramineae.

Habitat. The place of residence for plant, animal and other organism species.

Homologous chromosomes. A pair of chromosomes that are similar to each other in size, shape and the genes they carry.

Humus. The stable fraction of soil organic matter remaining after plant and animal decomposition.

Hydrosphere. The entire amount of water on the Earth. This includes water from the oceans, polar ice caps, surface waters on land, groundwater and water in the atmosphere.

Interspecific competition. Competition that occurs between two or more different species.

Intraspecific competition. Competition that occurs between individuals of the same species.

Isobar. A line passing through points on a weather map which have the same atmospheric pressure.

K-selection. Organisms able to compete at the carrying capacity of the habitat. K-selection weeds are able to compete in dense turfs and, compared to r-selected weeds, are physically larger and do not allocate considerable energy to reproduction.

Life history. An organism's life from birth or germination through growth and development to reproduction and death.

Light compensation point. The point where photosynthesis equals respiration.

Light-dependent reaction. The initial step in photosynthesis where sunlight is captured and energy compounds such as ATP are synthesized.

Light-independent reaction. The second step in photosynthesis where sugars and carbohydrates are manufactured using ATP.

Lignin. A complex strengthening material found in plants that is resistant to microbial breakdown.

Lithosphere. A general term for the solid portion of the Earth.

Macropore. A large soil pore that is considered the aeration pore since it is too large to hold moisture.

Mesophyll cells. The plant cells where most of the chloroplasts are found and consequently, where most of the photosynthesis occurs.

Microtubular spindle. Very small fibers that attach to chromosomes during nuclear division and help move the chromosomes to the proper cells.

Mitosis. Cell division in which the daughter cell contains the same chromosomes as the mother cell.

Mix. A combination of two or more grass species.

Multiple resistance. An organism that is resistant to two or more pesticides.

Multisite activity. Refers to the mode of action of a pesticide. A multisite pesticide disrupts the growth and leads to the death of a pest by interfering in more than one metabolic reaction.

Niche. The limits defined by both abiotic and biotic factors for growth, development and reproduction of a species.

Nitrification. The oxidation of ammonium to nitrate by soil microorganisms.

Northern Hemisphere. The part of the Earth north of the equator to the north pole.

Organic soil. A soil that contains a significant percentage, usually greater than 20 percent, organic matter throughout the profile.

Osmotic. A pressure that develops between two solutions containing unequal concentration of salts separated by a cell wall or membrane. Water will move from a low salt solution to a higher salt solution.

Overseed. The practice of seeding a dormant turfgrass, normally a warm-season species, with a turfgrass, normally a cool-season species, to provide color.

Oxidant. A substance that combines with oxygen.

Parent material. An unconsolidated mineral base from which soils develop.

Particle size. The diameter of a particle.

Pathogen. An organism that is capable of inciting a disease.

Permanent wilting point. The point where sufficient water for plant growth is not available in the soil.

Pest. Any organism/species that is considered undesirable in a turfgrass stand because it may cause disruption and death to the turfgrass plants. Pests are referred to as weeds, destructive insects and pathogens.

pH. A measure of the acidity or alkalinity of a solution using a scale from 1 to 14.

Photoperiodism. The response of organisms, flowering and germination, to the relative length of daily periods of light and darkness.

Photosynthesis. The capturing and converting of solar energy by plants into usable forms; the storing of energy in molecules derived from carbon dioxide and water.

Phytochrome. A light sensitive pigment that triggers hormone activity governing leaf expansion, stem branching, seed germination and flowering.

Population. A group of individuals of the same species found in a habitat.

Power rule. In reference to the slope of the self-thinning line biomass increases at a greater rate than density.

Primary mineral. A mineral that has remained unchanged from its inception. Sand and some forms of silt are examples of primary minerals.

Protein. An essential part of living cells composed of amino acids and linked in chains.

Quiescent. A lack of growth due to unfavorable environmental conditions. Once favorable conditions occur, growth resumes.

Relative humidity. A percentage of the maximum available water vapor moisture that the air can hold at a given temperature.

Resource. An item that can be consumed by an individual and, as a result, become unavailable to another organism.

R-selection. An organism containing traits that allow it to multiply rapidly. R-selection results in plants, like annual weeds, that reproduce profusely and quickly.

Resource depletion zone. The area around a plant in which the availability of a resource is reduced.

Respiration. Energy release from the breakdown of carbohydrates ending with the evolution of oxygen.

Runoff. The portion of precipitation that is lost from an area without entering the soil.

S

Scalping. The process where an excessive amount of green tissue is removed from the turfgrass stand by mowing. The effect is a brownish appearing turf. Physiologically, scalping may require considerable energy spent by the plant to regenerate new tissue.

Secondary mineral. A mineral that has undergone chemical change from weathering since its inception. Clay and some forms of silt are examples of secondary minerals.

Seed. A mature ovule containing a food source and surrounded by a protective coat.

Self Pollination. Pollen from the same plant fertilizes the egg.

Self-thinning. In plants, the inverse relationship between biomass and density which occurs at full canopy cover. As a population continues to grow and develop, it is at the expense of density (some individuals die).

Shade. A reduction in either quantity or quality of light intercepted by turfgrasses. Shade may be a result of trees, physical structures or neighboring turfgrass plants.

Sigmoid curve. An "s-shaped curve" that commonly represents an organism's growth. The curve has an initial acceleration phase followed by a deceleration phase leading to a leveling off.

Site-specific activity. Refers to a pesticide's mode of action. A site-specific pesticide disrupts the growth which leads to the death of a pest by interfering in one metabolic reaction.

Soil organic matter. The portion of the soil that includes plant and animal residues at various stages of decomposition.

Soil seed bank. The population of viable, but dormant seeds found in the soil.

Solar radiation. Energy arriving from the sun in the form of electromagnetic radiation. This energy is stored in plants through photosynthesis and as heat in the air, water or soil.

Southern hemisphere. The portion of the Earth south of the equator to the South pole.

Species. A population whose members interbreed and produce fertile offspring.

Spore. In fungi, an asexual reproductive cell that gives rise to hyphae. In plants, a haploid female or male gamete.

Stand. A group of turfgrass plants growing in a continuous area.

Stems. Components of the grass plant that give rise to new shoots including crowns, culm, rhizomes and stolons.

Stomates. Tiny passages in the leaf that allow for carbon dioxide exchange and water loss via transpiration.

Stress. In biology stress can mean many things including reduced growth caused by some condition. Stress is often used redundantly; for example, drought stress. In this text, stress is an all encompassing term used to describe a plant response that deviates from the norm.

Suppressive organism. An organism that reduces the ability of another organism to cause plant damage (i.e., pathogen). Sometimes referred to in this text as an antagonistic organism.

Synergism. In this text, synergism is used primarily to describe the enhanced disease control activity achieved by combining two fungicides, which is greater than each fungicide used alone.

Thatch. A partially decomposed organic layer that develops between the green vegetation and the soil surface. Thatch is resistant to decay, containing a significant amount of lignin from major components of thatch roots, stems and crowns.

Thunderstorm. A severe storm that is accompanied by lightning and thunder.

Tiller. A normally erect shoot that develops at ground level by grasses. Tillers are used as a means of quantifying turf density.

Transpiration. The loss of water from the leaf to the atmosphere through evaporation.

Turf. A term used to describe a turfgrass community that is mowed.

Turfgrass. A grass species maintained as a mowed turf.

Urease. An enzyme that catalyzes the reaction of urea to ammonia.

Vigor. A rather nebulous term used here in reference to seed vigor. The Association of Official Seed Analysts defines vigor as "those seed properties which determine the potential for rapid uniform emergence and development of normal seedlings under a wide range of field conditions."

Warm-season turfgrass. A turfgrass species that has an optimum temperature for growth between 80 and 95 F. Examples of warm-season turfgrasses include zoysiagrasses, bermudagrasses, centipedegrasses, St. Augustinegrasses and carpetgrasses.

Wave cyclone. A traveling vortex-like cyclone that involves the interaction of cold and warm air masses along fronts.

Wavelength. The distance between two successive waves measured from wave crest to wave crest. For light, wavelength is measured in nanometers which equals 0.04 millionths of an inch.

Wear. Injury to turfgrass plants caused by traffic such as equipment and human activities.

Weather. The state of the atmosphere at a given time and place.

Wetland. Wet, vegetated areas normally located between the yearly normal water line and the yearly normal flood water level.

Index

B

bermudagrass, 23, 24, 30, 34, 40, 54, 62, 67, 68, 71, 89, 102, 128, 131-133, 146, 153
billbug, 70, 98
biological agents, 143, 151
biological oxygen demand, 61
biological control, 114
biomass, 83, 103-110, 117, 141
boundary layer, 50, 64
brown patch, 92, 102, 145-146
browntop millet, 122
Buchloe dactyloides, 24, 69, 71
buffalograss, 24, 69, 71
bulk density, 80, 82-83, 87

C3 plants, 30, 40
C4 plants, 30, 40
calcareous soils, 85
canopy biomass, 32-33
capillary water, 79, 80, 88
carbohydrates, 65
carbon dioxide, 29, 38-40, 149
carpetgrass, 85
carrying capacity (K), 97, 99, 106, 109, 125
cation exchange capacity, 77, 78, 87
centipedegrass, 34, 54, 62, 71, 89, 122, 153
chickweed, 137
chilling injury, 68
chinchbug, 73, 99, 110, 119
chronic temperature stress
clay, 42, 76
cold hardiness, 68
cold front, 18
compaction (soil compaction), 53, 77, 135
companion grass, 122
complexity, 95
condensation, 51
convection, 16, 63
cool-season grass, 20, 63, 67-69, 71, 73, 83, 121, 129-132, 138
copper spot, 101
core cultivation, 83, 128, 133

Coriolus versicolor, 89,
crabgrass, 52, 123-126, 128, 131, 136-137, 147
creeping bentgrass, 23, 31, 34, 37, 41, 52, 54, 62, 71, 94, 117, 123-124, 128, 131-136, 138, 141, 142, 145, 150, 153
cultivar, 87, 104, 122, 131, 132, 140-141, 143-145, 150, 153
cultivation pan, 84
curly dock, 136
cyclone, 13, 16
Cynodon dactylon, 23, 24, 30, 34, 40, 54, 62, 67, 68, 71, 89, 102, 128, 131-133, 146, 153

dandelion, 126, 127, 130, 136-137
day-neutral plant, 31
deacclimation, 69
denaturation, 64
denitrification, 39, 42, 88, 149
density dependent, 95, 96 124
density, 95, 96 103-111, 117, 124-126, 130, 141, 148
dew, 50-51
dicarboximides, 112-113
disturbances, 94, 139, 148
dithiocarbamates, 112
dollar spot, 92, 101, 112, 113, 118, 145, 146
dormancy, summer, 53, 67
dormancy, winter, 67
Drechslera poae, 96
drought, 53, 131
drought resistance, 52-53
drought avoidance, 53
drought tolerance, 53

earthworms, 87, 89, 91
ecosystem, 11, 93, 129, 138, 142-143, 149
electrical conductivity, 57, 61
endophyte 104, 116, 145
enhanced degradation, 147-148, 152

Eremochloa ophiuroides, 34, 54, 62, 71, 89, 122, 153
evapotranspiration, 14, 15, 52, 55, 59, 66, 82

far-red wavelength, 26, 31-33
fertilizers, 43, 45, 56, 87, 99, 105, 145, 150
Festuca arundinacea, 24, 37, 52, 62, 71, 73, 83, 104, 116-117, 130, 131, 138, 141, 153
flooding, 54, 148
flurprimidol, 133
foxtail, 136-137
frost, 24
fungi, 91, 100, 111-112, 114, 143, 147, 151
fungicides, 87, 105, 110-114, 118, 147, 151-52

Gause hypothesis, 94
gene for gene, 143, 144
germination, 32-34, 41-42, 104-105, 125, 136
gibberellin, 28, 30
glycolysis, 27-28
goosegrass, 118, 131, 136-37
greenhouse effect, 38-40, 149
groundwater, 55
growing degree-day, 70, 72, 95
growth regulators, 133, 141, 150
grubs, 89, 145
guttation, 51
gypsum, 87

habitat, 75, 93, 97, 99, 106, 124-127, 130, 135
hail, 16, 22
heat shock proteins, 65
herbicides, 67, 110, 118, 126, 132-133, 146, 148, 151-152

heterozygous, 115
high pressure water injection, 84
high pressure, 13, 15, 23, 65
hollow tine, 83-84
homozygous, 115, 144
hydric soil, 149
hydrology cycle, 55
hydrophobic soils, 86
hydrosphere, 11, 13

insecticide, 110, 114-115, 119, 146, 151, 152
integrated pest management (IPM), 143
iprodione, 112, 114, 118, 152
irrigation, 52, 55-56, 130, 134-135
isobars, 12, 13
isobutylidene diurea (IBDU), 44

Japanese beetles, 70, 92, 119, 145
jet stream, 14

K selecting species, 125-127, 129, 136
Kentucky bluegrass, 31, 33-34, 37, 52, 54, 62, 71, 73, 82-83, 94, 105, 117, 121-123, 125,
    130, 134-135, 138, 140-141, 144, 146-147, 150, 153
knotweed, 136
Krebs cycle, 28

L

lambsquarter, 118, 136-137
leaching, 39, 42-43, 55, 86
leaf spot, 101, 142
light dependent reaction, 26-27
light compensation point
light independent reaction, 26-27, 29
lithosphere, 11, 13
logistic growth, 96
Lolium perenne, 23, 31, 34, 37, 41, 62, 71, 83, 104-105, 116-117, 121, 123, 128, 131-133, 138, 146, 147, 153
Lolium multiflorum, 24, 71, 118, 141, 153
long-day plant, 31-32
low pressure, 13-14

M

mercury, 36, 151
microorganisms, 88, 91, 147
milky spore disease, 145
mineralization, 39, 40-42
moisture, 17, 19, 23, 32, 104, 108, 135
moisture stress, 50
monsoon, 15
mowing, 87, 94, 103, 107-110, 123-126, 132-133, 139-141, 145, 150

N

necrotic ring spot, 92, 102, 130
nematode, 89, 91, 145, 151
net radiation, 63
niche, 93, 134-135
nitrate, 39, 42-43, 45, 131
nitrogen cycle, 39-40, 149

nitrogen, 36, 40-46, 48, 109, 110, 122, 130-132, 134-135, 148
non-target, 146-147
nutsedge, 137

organic matter 76
oscillation, 99, 110
osmotic drought, 54
overseeding, 68, 105, 131-132
oxygen diffusion rates 36
oxygen, 35-36, 135
ozone, 36-38

paclobutrazol, 141, 150
Paspalum notatum, 59, 71
pathogens, 89, 96-98, 103, 110-112, 139, 142-147
peat, 82
perennial ryegrass, 23, 31, 34, 37, 41, 62, 71, 83, 104-105, 116-117, 121, 123, 128, 131-133, 138, 146, 147, 153
pesticide resistance, 111, 124
pesticides, 56, 87, 89, 110-112, 114, 124, 143, 145-148, 151, 152
pH, 84, 87
Phebia gigantea, 89
phosphorus, 36, 41, 42, 45-47, 122, 134, 135
photoperiod, 30-32, 67, 68
photorespiration, 29, 30, 133
photosynthesis, 15, 25-30, 32, 33, 35, 37-39, 49, 63, 64, 67
phytochrome 32, 33, 106,
plant host resistance, 143-144
plantain, 136, 137
poa annua, 31, 34, 37, 41, 52, 54, 62, 71, 73, 83, 94, 118, 122-124, 126-132, 134-138, 140-141, 150
poa pratensis, 31, 33-34, 37, 52, 54, 62, 71, 73, 82-83, 94, 105, 117, 121-123, 125, 130, 134-135, 138, 140-141, 144, 146-147, 150, 153
population size, 93, 97, 99, 125

thistle, 136-137
thunderstorms, 15-16, 18-19
tillering, 31-32, 103, 106
tillers, 103-104, 106-107
tillering capacity, 122-124, 129
Tilman's model, 133, 136
topdressing, 81, 83, 133
traffic, 80-82, 94
transpiration, 29, 38, 49-50, 53, 63-64
tropical cyclone, 16
2-4,D, 143, 147, 152

ultra-violet light
urea, 41-45, 48
ureaformeldehyde, 43-44
urease, 41-42

vapor pressure gradient, 49
vertical mowing, 133
volatilization 39, 41-43

warm-season grass, 20, 63, 67-69, 71, 122, 131-133
warm front, 18
water insoluble nitrogen (WIN), 44
water-holding capacity, 53, 77, 79
water quality, 55
water-use rate, 51-52
wave cyclones, 18-19
wear tolerance, 40, 83, 109, 117, 141
weeds, 110, 124-126, 128-130, 132, 136-138, 141-143, 146-148
wet wilt, 28, 35, 37, 53
wetland, 140, 146, 148, 149